IMAGING IDENTITY
MEDIA, MEMORY AND PORTRAITURE IN THE DIGITAL AGE

IMAGING IDENTITY

MEDIA, MEMORY AND PORTRAITURE IN THE DIGITAL AGE

EDITED BY MELINDA HINKSON

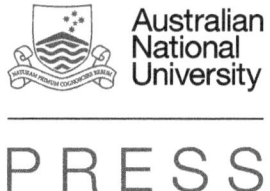

PRESS

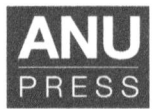

Published by ANU Press
The Australian National University
Acton ACT 2601, Australia
Email: anupress@anu.edu.au
This title is also available online at press.anu.edu.au

National Library of Australia Cataloguing-in-Publication entry

Title: Imaging identity : media, memory and portraiture in the digital age / Melinda Hinkson.

ISBN: 9781760460402 (paperback) 9781760460419 (ebook)

Subjects: Portraits.
Personality and culture.
Digital images.
Computer art.

Other Creators/Contributors:
Hinkson, Melinda, editor.

Dewey Number: 757

All rights reserved. No part of this publication may be reproduced, stored in a retrieval system or transmitted in any form or by any means, electronic, mechanical, photocopying or otherwise, without the prior permission of the publisher.

Cover design and layout by ANU Press.
Cover photograph: *Autumn song* (still) by John Conomos.

This edition © 2016 ANU Press

*Dedicated to the memory of Andrew Sayers (1957–2015),
inaugural director of the National Portrait Gallery of Australia,
whose creative thinking and great friendship inspired the
scholarly activity that led to this book.*

Contents

List of figures ix
Acknowledgements xiii
Contributors xv
Introduction: The time of the portrait is now 1
Melinda Hinkson

PART I: The work of the imagination

1. Rembrandt, or the portrait as encounter 15
   Didier Maleuvre
2. Pictures for our time and place: Reflections on painting
   in a digital age 37
   Melinda Hinkson
3. Diasporic looking: Portraiture, diaspora and subjectivity 59
   Gali Weiss

PART II: Interfaces

4. The self-portrait and the film and video essay 85
   John Conomos
5. The mutable face 101
   Michele Barker and Anna Munster
6. BarkTV: Portrait of an innovator 117
   Jennifer Deger

Index 141

List of figures

Figure 1.1: *Portrait of Johannes Wtenbogaert* (detail), Rembrandt Harmensz. van Rijn, 1633, 130 x 103 cm 19

Figure 1.2: *Self-portrait as the Apostle Paul*, Rembrandt Harmensz. van Rijn, 1661, oil on canvas, 91 x 77 cm 30

Figure 2.1: Left: *Boatmen moored on a lakeshore*, Adam Pynacker, 1668; Right: *Proposal for landscaped cosmos*, Sam Leach, 2010. 39

Figure 2.2: *Untitled #2*, from the series *Yooralla at twenty past three*, Micky Allan, 1978, watercolour and coloured pencil on silver gelatin print, 27.7 x 35.2 cm 45

Figure 2.3: *Large interior 173 (Micky)*, Jude Rae, 2005, oil on linen, 180 x 120 cm, winner of the 2005 Portia Geach Memorial Award for portraiture 48

Figure 2.4: *Drawing 101 (naked)*, Jude Rae, 2010, willow charcoal on Fabriano paper, 220 x 140 cm 50

Figure 2.5: *Sorcery painting (autumn echidna)*, Vanessa Barbay, 2011, echidna and rabbit-skin glue on canvas, 84 x 80 cm ... 52

Figure 3.1: *An ocean of bright clouds, an ocean of solemn clouds*, Lindy Lee, 1995, photocopy and acrylic on board, 205 x 143 cm 67

Figure 3.2: *Birth & death*, Lindy Lee, 2003, Installation Artspace, Sydney, inkjet print and acrylic on Chinese accordion books, installation dimensions variable 68

Figure 3.3: *Aaron*, Gali Weiss, 2000, solvent transfer, charcoal, graphite, 76 x 56.5 cm 71

Figure 3.4: *MotherDaughter (as self-portrait)*, Gali Weiss, 2008, watercolour, solvent transfer, charcoal, graphite, 75 x 75 cm each of 6 panels 73

Figure 3.5: *FatherDaughter*, Gali Weiss, 2008, ink and watercolour wash, solvent transfer, charcoal, graphite, 52.5 x 37 cm each of 14 panels 75

Figure 3.5a: *FatherDaughter* (detail), Gali Weiss, 2008, ink and watercolour wash, solvent transfer, charcoal, graphite, 52.5 x 37 cm each of 14 panels 75

Figure 3.6: *MotherSon*, Gali Weiss, 2008, solvent transfer, graphite, 37 x 30 cm each of 15 panels 76

Figure 3.7: *MotherSon II*, Gali Weiss, 2008, black & white and colour solvent transfer, 60 x 40.5 cm each of four panels 78

Figure 3.8: *MotherSon III*, Gali Weiss, 2008, black & white and colour solvent transfer, 60 x 40.5 cm each panel. 81

Figure 4.1: *Autumn song* (still), John Conomos, 1998, SP Beta, 23 mins duration 98

Figure 4.2: *The spiral of time* (still), John Conomos, 2013, HD video, 5 minutes duration 100

Figure 5.1: Photographic montage depicting different facial expressions induced by electrical currents 102

Figures 5.2 and 5.3: The facial expression of fear being induced by electrical currents 106

Figure 5.4: Horror and agony 107

Figure 5.5: Terror 107

Figure 5.6: *Duchenne's smile* (still), two-channel video installation, Michele Barker and Anna Munster, 2009 109

Figure 6.1: *Portrait of Ugolino Martelli*, Angelo *Bronzino*, 1536 or 1537, oil on wood, oil on poplar wood 119

Figure 6.2: *Djalkiri #1*, David Bukulatjpi, Jennifer Deger and Marrawakamirr Marrawungu, 2009, video and acrylic on bark. 119

Figure 6.3: *Djalkiri #1*, Macquarie University Art Gallery, December 2009. 120

Figure 6.4: *Djalkiri #1* (detail) 123

Figure 6.5: Jennifer Deger and Bangana Wununungmurra in the BRACS radio studio, Gapuwiyak 1999 125

Figure 6.6: *Family portrait #3, Christmas Birrimbirr* (Christmas spirit), installation, Miyarrka Media, 2011 126

Figure 6.7: *Christmas with Wawa* (still), Jennifer Deger with Susan Marrawakamirr Marrawungu, 2007 126

Figure 6.8: The entrance to Bangana Wunungmurra's funeral shade, 2001 127

Figure 6.9: Portrait of father and daughter, 2005 128

Figure 6.10: Studio portrait of Susan Marrawakamirr Marrawungu and Bangana Wunungmurra, 1997 129

Figure 6.11: Family portrait at grave, 2007 132

Figure 6.12: David Bukulatjpi painting *Djalkiri #1*, 2009 133

Figure 6.13: Portrait of Bangana Wunungmurra, date unknown.. 134

Figure 6.14: *ONLY.FAMILY*, Rowena Lay'pu Wunungmurra, 2010, phone-made jpeg 135

Figure 6.15: *Djalkiri #1* (close-up), during test projections, 2009 .. 136

Figure 6.16: Jennifer Deger, Samantha Yawulwuy Wunungmurra, Antonnio Gurruruu Wanambi, Susan Marrawakamirr Marrawungu, Macquarie University Art Gallery 2009 139

Acknowledgements

This book had its origins in an international symposium hosted in July 2010 by Australia's National Portrait Gallery, the year it opened its new premises in Canberra. The idea for a conference exploring intersections between portraiture and identity in the digital age came about in conversations with the inaugural director of the Gallery, the late Andrew Sayers. Pamela Clelland Gray was an enthusiastic co-convenor of the symposium. We enjoyed additional support from ANU colleagues Caroline Turner and Howard Morphy, and from Louise Doyle and Michael Desmond of the National Portrait Gallery, who curated the temporary exhibition 'Present Tense' to coincide with the symposium.

I thank all contributors for their patience in watching this book come to fruition. I am particularly grateful to the artists who have generously allowed their works to be reproduced in the pages that follow—Micky Allan, Vanessa Barbay, Lindy Lee, Jude Rae—as well as to Roslyn Oxley9 Gallery and the Rijksmuseum, Amsterdam. I also thank those contributors whose own creative works are included in this volume—Michele Barker and Anna Munster, John Conomos, Jennifer Deger and the Miyarrka Media collective, and Gali Weiss. Special thanks are given to John Conomos for permission to reproduce a photographic still from his *Autumn Song* (1998) as the book's cover image.

Alison Caddick has brought her characteristic sharp eye and thoughtful way with words to the process of copyediting. Staff at ANU Press have been efficient and supportive in dealing with images, design and production issues.

Finally, production of this book has benefited from the support of an ANU Press publication subsidy as well as a research dissemination grant from the Alfred Deakin Institute, Deakin University.

Contributors

Michele Barker is an artist and academic who works in the field of new media. She has developed still image, video and interactive projects addressing processes of perception, embodiment and scientific/medical visualisation. Her work has been exhibited widely in Australia and internationally, including at Vidarte, the Mexican Biennale of Video Art, MOCA Taipei and the Art Gallery of New South Wales. She regularly collaborates with artist and new media theorist Anna Munster. Arising out of a residency at Eyebeam, New York, they developed the award-wining multichannel work *Struck*, which has been exhibited in Australia, the US, China and Taiwan. Also in collaboration with Munster, Barker created *évasion* (2014), a responsive installation working between dance, performance and the moving image; and *HokusPokus* (2011), which explores the relationships between perception, magic and early moving-image technologies and techniques. This work was chosen to represent Australasia at the International Festival of Digital Art as part of the London Cultural Olympiad and London 2012 Festival. Michele is a senior lecturer at UNSW Art & Design.

John Conomos is an associate professor and principal fellow at Victorian College of the Arts, University of Melbourne. An artist and writer who works across a number of media forms—video, film, installation, photography and radiophonic art—he has exhibited widely in Australia, and overseas in the US, the UK, France, Germany, Latin America, Canada and Greece. John is a New Media Fellow of the Australia Council for the Arts and a prolific contributor to art, film and cultural theory journals. He is the author and co-editor of numerous books. His most recent co-edited book, with Brad Buckley, *Erasure: The spectre of cultural memory* (Libri Publishing, UK) was published in 2015. At present John is working on a new collection with Brad Buckley, *A companion to curation* (Wiley-Blackwell, forthcoming), and a mixed-media exhibition, *Paging Mr Hitchcock*, for the Mosman Art Gallery, Sydney.

Jennifer Deger is an anthropologist, a filmmaker and research leader at the Cairns Institute, James Cook University. Her practice-led research explores the role of digital technologies in social transformation. Jennifer has published widely on Aboriginal visual culture, experimental ethnography and the anthropology of art and Indigenous aesthetics. Her creative projects with the collective Miyarrka Media include the films *Manapanmirr, in Christmas spirit* (2012) and *Ringtone* (2014); video artworks *My red Yolngu heart* (2011) and *Christmas with Wawa* (2008); and the exhibition projects *Christmas Birrimbirr (Christmas spirit)* (2011) and *Gapuwiyak calling: Phone-made media from Arnhem Land* (2014). She is currently co-authoring a book with Miyarrka Media about mobile phones and the Aboriginal art of connection.

Melinda Hinkson is an associate professor of anthropology and Australian Research Council Future Fellow in the Alfred Deakin Institute for Citizenship and Globalisation, Deakin University, and visiting fellow in the School of Archaeology and Anthropology, The Australian National University. She has published widely on Warlpiri engagements with visual media, on the life work of Australian anthropologist WEH Stanner, on the contested cultural politics of the Northern Territory Intervention, and on the broader field of contemporary cultural attitudes to images. Her most recent publications are *Remembering the future: Warlpiri life through the prism of drawing* (Aboriginal Studies Press, 2014), and an associated exhibition, *Warlpiri drawings: Remembering the future,* at the National Museum of Australia, August 2014 – June 2015, and Charles Darwin University Gallery, August–October 2015.

Didier Maleuvre is professor of Comparative Literature at the University of California, Santa Barbara. He has been a visiting professor in Holland and Argentina, and has lectured widely in Europe, the Americas and Australia. Didier's area of research is the history of ideas, art and literature. He is the author of three books, the most recent being *The horizon: A history of our infinite longing* (California University Press, 2011). His forthcoming book is titled *The art of civilization: A bourgeois history* (Springer Palgrave Macmillan), which argues that art has served a demystifying function in western civilisation, advancing a rationalised (some would say disenchanted, others bourgeois) view of existence.

Anna Munster is an associate professor at UNSW Art & Design. Her recent book, *An aesthesia of networks: Conjunctive experience in art and technology* (Technologies of lived abstraction series, MIT Press, 2013) explores new expressions of networks beyond the 'link-node' image and new understandings of experience that account for the complexity of contemporary assemblages between humans and non-human technics. She is also the author of *Materializing new media: Embodiment in information aesthetics* (Dartmouth College Press, 2006). She is a founding member of the online, peer-reviewed journal *The Fibreculture Journal*, and has published in *Inflexions*, *CTheory*, *Culture Machine* and *Theory, Culture and Society*. Anna is a practising media artist, regularly collaborating with Michele Barker. Anna is particularly interested in the relation of sound, vision and movement in perception. Her recent artworks are listed in Michele Barker's biographical notes.

Gali Weiss is a Melbourne artist. Her past practice has centred on drawing installations and the artist's book. Currently it is focused on multimedia work, comprising drawing, printmaking and photomedia, and sound. She has a PhD from Victoria University for her practice-led research on portraiture and diaspora. Her work is represented in various public collections, including the National Gallery of Australia, the state libraries of Victoria and Queensland, the University of Melbourne and the Israel Museum.

Introduction: The time of the portrait is now

Melinda Hinkson

In December 2008, Australia celebrated the opening of a new national cultural institution. A striking new building in Canberra's parliamentary triangle declared portraiture to have achieved a rare political outcome: a $76 million building cemented the genre's status in our national consciousness. The process leading to the opening of this building had commenced a decade and a half earlier with the advocacy of arts philanthropists Gordon and Marilyn Darling and the mounting of a travelling exhibition, *Uncommon Australians: Towards an Australian national portrait gallery*, which opened at the National Gallery of Victoria and then toured to Canberra, Brisbane, Sydney and Adelaide. Funding was subsequently allocated to enable the establishment of a fledgling national portrait gallery in three rooms of Old Parliament House. In 1997, then Prime Minister John Howard declared his enthusiasm for a freestanding institution dedicated to portraiture and allocated the funds required to plan and erect the new building.[1] Portraiture was the art form that seemed to speak most compellingly to the cultural moment; in terms of the public politics fostered by Howard, the actions and achievements of individual 'great Australians', whether past prime ministers, cricket players, entrepreneurs or neighbourhood heroes, were to be lauded over 'lofty ideas' or 'culture'. In this context it was observed that the new institution enjoyed a dream run of political support and public acclaim.[2]

---

1   See 'Gallery history', National Portrait Gallery, www.portrait.gov.au/content/gallery-history/, nd, accessed 1 November 2015.
2   John Thompson, 'At the national portrait gallery: Art or history?', *Recollections*, vol. 5 no. 1, 2010, recollections.nma.gov.au/issues/vol_5_no_1/notes_and_comments/at_the_national_portrait_gallery_art_or_history, accessed 1 November 2015.

The government's backing of the gallery turned out to be an inspired move. People came in large numbers—300,000 passed through the doors in the first three months—and they have continued to come in good numbers since. Yet the reason for the gallery's success as a new place of the people may well rest on a more complex conjunction of factors than its champions had in mind.

Following the opening of the gallery, I wrote an essay in which I posed the question, 'What is this new institution?'

> Part of its interest and potential surely lies in its very ambiguity: this is not simply another fine art gallery, nor a museum in the conventional sense of the term ... the very idea of a portrait gallery built around the recognition of 'notable' individuals and their contribution to nation making has been scorned by some as an exercise in barren elitism, and the gallery's ambiguous status accused of giving rise to nothing more than a mix of 'bad history and inadequate psychology with inferior art'.[3] Yet such criticism seems to miss a fundamental point: this is a gallery born in an era of accelerated technological mediation. Part of the aim of the Gallery requires it to eschew the values of high art in favour of forms of image-making drawn from a wider public domain. In a society that measures social achievement in large part through a person's attainment of status *as* image, most often attended to in the form of the face, a portrait gallery is likely to have a particular appeal, especially for its direct engagement with the cult of celebrity, with forms of image culture that are embraced in the world beyond art galleries.[4]

In an age of digital mediation the portraiture recognised by and displayed within the art museum cannot but collide with and be shaped by a swirl of images and image-based practices that circulate beyond its doors. Faces of advertising and consumer culture, the reconfiguration of public/private spheres found in the new self-fashioning and presentation techniques of social networking,

---

3   Humphrey McQueen, 'In for "'higher art' I'd go" at the National Portrait Gallery', *Australian Book Review*, May 2009, pp. 41–3.
4   Melinda Hinkson, 'Seeing more than black and white: Picturing Aboriginality at Australia's National Portrait Gallery', *Australian Humanities Review*, no. 49, 2010, pp. 5–28.

a burgeoning industry in cosmetic surgery, the increase in surveillance technologies dealing in facial recognition all indicate a collective heightened attention to faces.[5]

From a diverse range of perspectives, the essays in this book consider why it is that portraits—pictures of faces—continue to have such galvanising appeal and perform such fundamental work across myriad social settings. In doing so, they look beyond conventional ideas of the portrait as a medium for celebrating individual and national achievement to the wider cultural contexts, governmental practices and intimate experiences that shape relationships between persons and pictures.

These essays have their origins in an international symposium held at the National Portrait Gallery in Canberra over three days in July 2010. Strongly interdisciplinary in its focus, that event brought together anthropologists, artists, art historians, literary and media scholars, and curators to explore a conjunction of interests and paradoxes at work in contemporary image-making practices and visual experience. While preserving the diversity of perspective and concerns of the 2010 symposium, the essays collected here also traverse considerable shared ground. They are written by artists, anthropologists, art historians and media scholars. At the heart of their collective concern is a commitment to understanding interactions between persons and images as an elemental component of what it is to be human, and to grapple with what is distinctive in such interactions in the present, a time when digital forms of imaging and interaction have become ubiquitous, contradictory, constitutive elements of everyday life.

Attending to the many ways in which identity is 'imaged' in the present, contributors find various degrees of analytical traction in the concept of portraiture. Portraiture has been crucial to the formation and articulation of modern individualism;[6] it might be seen as a primary genre through which the culture of western modernity has

---

5   Martyn Jolly, 'The face in digital space', in Anne Marsh, Melissa Miles and Daniel Palmer (eds), *The Culture of Photography in Public Space*, Bristol, Intellect, 2014, pp. 144–57; Justin Clemens and Adam Nash, 'Take a good hard look at yourself: Autoscopia and the networked image', in *New imaging: Transdisciplinary strategies for art beyond the new media*, Sydney, Australian Network for Art and Technology, 2011, pp. 40–51.
6   Joanna Woodall, *Portraiture: Facing the subject*, Manchester, Manchester University Press, 1997.

been animated and reinforced. As a genre of European art, portraiture is a well-travelled field.[7] Yet as Ernst van Alphen observes, artists have continued to push the boundaries of the medium as they have grappled with a changing world of human experience, and especially with the dislocation and diasporic experience that is a cornerstone of modernity. Just as what it is to be human has continued to be reshaped by technological intervention and other transformations in our world, artists have grappled with such change by re-imagining and reformulating the medium of portraiture. In the words of van Alphen, 'the project of "portraying somebody in her/his individuality or quality or essence" is no longer the sanctifying function of portraiture'. But this is not to say that portraiture is an exhausted medium; a genre can be liberated from its history.[8]

> The portrait returns but with a difference, now in order to expose the bourgeious self, historically anchored and naturalized, instead of its authority; to show a loss of self instead of its consolidation; to shape the subject as simulacrum instead of as origin.[9]

While not all contributors would agree with van Alphen's interpretation of the nature of contemporary subjectivity, they do agree that portraiture as a genre is necessarily remade to capture new kinds of persons and new perspectives on human experience in new times and places. In the essays that follow, this work occurs along four analytic fronts. Firstly, there is a decentring of focus from the object of portrayal (the authority of the sitter) to the effects of the picture, or in the words of philosopher Hans-Georg Gadamer, its 'increase of being'.[10] Secondly, there is an exploration of the medium from the inside: for practising artists, portraiture becomes an activity in autobiographical sense-making. Thirdly, portraiture and images of the face are taken up as a medium for exploring larger social relations; for example, the practices of governmentality and biopolitics that are

---

7   Richard Brilliant, *Portraiture: Essays in art and culture*, London, Reaktion Books, 1991; Woodall; Tony Halliday, *Facing the public: Portraiture in the aftermath of the French Revolution*, Manchester, Manchester University Press, 1999; Shearer West, *Portraiture*, Oxford, Oxford University Press, 2004; Stephen Perkinson, *The likeness of the King: A prehistory of portraiture in late medieval France*, Chicago, Chicago University Press, 2009; Cynthia Freeland, *Portraits and persons*, Oxford, Oxford University Press, 2010.
8   Ernst van Alphen, 'The portrait's dispersal', *Art in mind: How contemporary images shape thought*, Chicago, Chicago University Press, 2005, p. 47.
9   van Alphen, 2005, p. 25.
10 Cited in van Alphen, 2005, pp. 23–4.

seen to characterise our times.¹¹ And finally, anthropologists explore the elasticity of portraiture as a medium, testing the genre's capacity to convey ontologically different modes of personhood and relationships between human and other beings and the environments they inhabit.

While working from diverse disciplinary bases and with different materials and influences, all the contributors to this book are firmly focused upon the *intersubjective* space of the portrait image. In each of the essays, people are considered to enter into highly intimate and potentially transformative relations through images. In declaring 'the time of the portrait is now', Didier Maleuvre foregrounds the 'now of encounter', the moment of embodied meeting between person and picture. For artists/authors John Conomos and Gali Weiss, portraiture is approached as a practice through which shape and meaning might be given to elusive diasporic life trajectories. Jennifer Deger is more circumspect about the capacity of portraiture to capture the dense intergenerational and intercultural relations between persons, spirits and environment in eastern Arnhem Land, but the multi-mediated 'BarkTV' she produced with her Yolngu collaborators presents a compelling instantiation through which to contemplate such a constellation of relations. She alerts us to the difficulty of grappling with cross-cultural portraits, reminding us via Jean-Luc Nancy that while portraits are places of encounter between self and other, they 'await viewers already imprinted with the echo of encounter'. In other words, crucially, we have already learned how to look at pictures, and *what to look for* in them, before we come to gaze upon any particular portrait.

One avenue of consideration opened up somewhat differently in essays by Didier Maleuvre and Melinda Hinkson is the importance of distinguishing the material presence and 'still' pictures of painting from photographs and the 'fleeting' images we commonly confront in digital format on the screens of computers and mobile phones. Paintings 'allow us to reflect from a distance and visually grasp the whole',¹² whereas digital images travel before our eyes at speeds at which we can only grasp them partially, fleetingly. The distinction

---

11   Pasi Väliaho, *Biopolitical screens: Image, power and the neoliberal brain*, Cambridge, Massachusetts, MIT Press, 2014.
12   Väliaho, 2014, p. 12; Siri Hudsvedt, *Mysteries of the rectangle*, New York, Princeton Architectural, 2005.

between these two differently structured visual experiences marks a crucial element of portraiture's crisis, and simultaneously its renewed interest for the contributors to this volume.

Didier Maleuvre responds provocatively to our concern with the specificity of the digital. The time of the portrait is now, he declares, but the portrait he champions is not the transforming and fleeting digital image but rather the classical, painted portraiture of Rembrandt. He finds the special potency of Rembrandt's portraits in the nature of encounter they call out between viewer and painting, as well as the fragility they convey. Drawing our attention to the cultural context in which Rembrandt's commissions were produced, Maleuvre observes the 'pained need for confirmation' in these 'faces of people who lived by the esteem of others'. Rembrandt's portraiture distils a significant moment of social transformation when an emergent merchant class looked to secure public recognition. Thus, Maleuvre suggests, Rembrandt's picture-making marks the emergence of acknowledgement-based identity in the Netherlands—the coming into being of the social gaze that lies at the heart of modern European subjectivity. Rembrandt's portraits do not *observe* but rather *recommend* a face for our attention. Rembrandt's method turns upon 'a labour of becoming acquainted' involving months of grappling in paint with a sitter's face. For Maleuvre, Rembrandt's paintings call out mutuality.

Didier Maleuvre juxtaposes this dense painterly activity with the practice of photography, which lacks duration. Photography's incapacity to 'wait on the face' cannot produce portraits. Here Maleuvre articulates the ultimate moral argument for distinguishing technological modes of mediation: while the practice of painting provides a vehicle for the sustained care of the other, photography is distracted, fleeting, superficial; it turns away, calling on technical skills, not human engagement. The portrait, Maleuvre concludes, 'is a modality of human solidarity' and thus the term must be reserved for the medium of paint and activity required of it.

For artists/writers, such distinctions between media are not necessarily so straightforward. Moving between and across the methods of drawing, painting, photography and video, artists often adopt a variety of practices and processes as a means to work through problems. Such practices of sense-making are highly intimate and evolve organically, but are also rigorously tested against a wider field of ideas and scholarship. Melinda Hinkson's essay explores these processes at work in the practice of three Canberra-based artists, all of whom identify first and foremost as painters. In this ethnographic engagement with artists in their studios, photography emerges as technical prop, as escape from the intensity of painting and also as facilitator of human interaction and the making of portraits. In watching painters wrestle with the challenge of creative work—with the conundrum of how to make something that is absent present in the form of a picture—the interplay between photography, on the one hand, and the hand-based practices of painting and drawing, on the other, emerges as vital and highly contingent. In one case, the intervention of photography is essential to artist Jude Rae's being able to gain sufficient distance on her subject to produce a satisfactory picture. For Micky Allan, photography facilitates creative social interaction in a period when painting is difficult and alienating. For Vanessa Barbay, the use of scanner and projector in the making of pictures that speak back to abstract engagements between persons and animals is a necessary compromise to help her meet the formal requirements of her PhD painting program. These intimate glimpses of creative work reveal that portrait-making cannot but shadow the artist's own subjectivity. The works and working methods of Allan, Barbay and Rae show image-making to be a product of habitus,[13] the location of the enactment of personhood where life experience and social constraints come together in processes of mutual constitution.

Artist and writer Gali Weiss explores portraiture as a medium for grappling with her own and others' diasporic subjectivities. Drawing on the work of Stuart Hall, Weiss adopts a view of diasporic experience as a constant process of becoming through creative action—a form of *identification*, rather than identity. Diasporic experience is necessarily intersubjective: it 'cannot be represented from the viewpoint of one-point perspective'. The space of diaspora encompasses 'those who leave as well as those who stay and those who return'. Taking that observation as a central force in her work, Weiss has developed a portrait practice that incorporates this 'doubling reference', producing pictures that distil the relationship between a sitter and an absent relative, as well as herself as image-maker. Working between the media

---

13   Pierre Bourdieu, *Outline of a theory of practice*, Cambridge, Cambridge University Press, 1977.

of photography, photocopying and drawing, Weiss' portraits become meeting places—of two individuals separated by space yet connected by a shared history of familial and emotional ties, brought together in the activity of making the picture. Art, and portrait-making in particular, are regarded here not as representation but rather as performative agency.

The digital is a crucial medium for Weiss' mode of exploration, as it is also for Chinese-Australian artist Lindy Lee, with whose work Weiss closely identifies. In Lee's portraits, the photocopy works as a metaphor for the diasporic experience of unbelonging and cultural displacement—the impossibility of reaching the 'original'. Lee speaks back to the conventional portrait and the illusion of the authentic subject it celebrates, appropriating images of European Old Master portraits and reworking their clarity and their visibility. New modes of identification and experience as well as indeterminate futures are attended to once the space of portraiture is reconfigured to shadow the space of diaspora.

John Conomos reflects upon four decades of his own film- and video-making and the evolution of a mode of practice consonant with his 'poly-cultural' or 'hybrid alien' Greek-Australian identifications. In this deeply personal essay, Conomos tracks his adoption of the video or film essay as the truest, most open creative form in which to wrestle with and express who he is. He gives us the image of himself as a small boy hanging about in his parents' suburban milk bar, watching the doorway that would 'magically transform into a movie screen, a world of enchantment' as he waited for the next customer. For Conomos the diasporic experience of being in-between calls out a distinctive imagination and need to write and make films as acts of 'interior emigration'.

In declaring the video essay as his chosen mode of self-portraiture or autobiography, Conomos adopts a practice of creative exploration that is at once intimate and 'dear', yet theoretically significant. In the presentation of his life trajectory, we witness not an unfolding of technological developments but rather a splicing of the analogue and digital as 'one continuous dialogue of art-making'. Conomos pays homage to Montaigne's idea of the essay as a vehicle for 'speculating aloud and testing ideas on paramount questions of life, culture, politics, human fragility and society', with what he sees as a play between 'fact and fiction' that later writers such as Georg Lukacs and Theodor Adorno honed into an aesthetic that privileged 'fragmentary, wandering concerns and stylistics'. Imagination, the unreliability of memory and pastiche are all crucial elements of Conomos' production. In his work the portrait emerges as a highly elastic and fluid set of traces: blurred images of encounters and experiences, lines of text, sequences of film, the influences of absent persons, his own mimetic performances—enfolded in the video essay. There is a strong moral element to Conomos' work that references artists, scholars and filmmakers of earlier eras as an 'antidote' to what he sees as 'the underlying institutionalised amnesia' characterising much of the contemporary interest in 'new' media. While his approach as 'rag-picker' gives him a predilection for seeing a continuous flow between and across forms of media, he nevertheless wants to make visible the history of genre and form that informs such intertextuality. Consequently, Conomos' images lead the viewer away from their surfaces, tracking art and life as a form of personalised interrogation of the past.

Michele Barker and Anna Munster take us to another, related field of exploration in their examination of the links between nineteenth-century scientific pursuits and contemporary adaptations of facial-imaging techniques. They do this by way of their own video installation, *Duchenne's smile*. The subject matter of this work are certain photographs in Charles Darwin's 1872 *The expression of the emotions in man and animals*, and in particular a series made by neurologist Guillaume-Benjamin-Amand Duchenne, who photographed his own experiments with electrical stimulation of facial muscles of patients suffering from various neurological conditions. Taking up the camera when the technology was in its infancy, Duchenne's experiments required him to work with long shutter speeds. He thus devised techniques to prolong the electrically charged expressions on his patients' faces so that they could be captured, making their responses conform to the technical constraints of the camera. Michele Barker and Anna Munster draw our attention to the doubled process by which a scientist would experiment with a technical treatment for an affliction at the same time as ensuring that the results of his experiments were recordable and thus visible to his peers. Drawing a link from Duchenne's experiments to contemporary facial-recognition software, Barker and Munster explore the incorporation of a typology of emotions into the workings of diverse corporate, governmental and policing practices.

Digitisation has been crucial to these developments, enabling the rise of a new biopolitics in which the face 'becomes *the* dominant surface for tracking, tracing and controlling the subject'.

Along with the other contributors to this volume who see the portrait as a genre ceaselessly being refigured across time and space to grapple with distinctive and evolving forms of personhood, Barker and Munster observe how the 'the abstract machine of faciality', as elucidated by Gilles Deleuze and Félix Guattari, is refigured, made subject to new techniques and technologies as new circumstances arise. They observe in the post-9/11 security environment an extraordinary expansion of the application of facial-recognition techniques. The developments they track call to mind the work of WJT Mitchell,[14] who identifies images as living organisms and argues that a recent biocybernetic turn in imaging has supplanted earlier representational modes. Endorsing this interpretation, Pasi Väliaho has recently written that 'images today proliferate and evolve in parallel with the production and promotion of the neoliberal way of life, with its notions of threat, contingency and emergency'.[15]

As they trace echoes of Duchenne's experiment in the workings of present-day surveillance technologies, Barker and Munster reveal the distinctive regime of truth constructed for reading emotions, a regime that operates entirely at the level of technological abstraction. This is the real-world nightmare of securitisation, which dovetails with Maleuvre's critique of photography.

The final essay in this volume draws our concerns with the intersubjective nature of person–image relations into the space of cross-cultural collaboration. Jennifer Deger revisits the process of producing, with her long-term Yolngu research associates and adoptive family, a 'BarkTV' to honour the remarkable intercultural life and legacy of their deceased husband, father and adoptive brother, Dhalwangu community leader and media maker, Bangana, who died suddenly in 2002. *Djalkiri #1* is a multimedia work, a bark painting in acrylic, the first of its kind produced at Gapuwiak, and even more unusual, incorporating a blank panel through the middle—a screen

---

14   WJT Mitchell, *What do pictures want? The lives and loves of images*, Chicago, Chicago University Press, 2005.
15   Väliaho, 2014, p. xii.

onto which video footage is projected of the headstone-laying ceremony that completed the formal period of mourning for this man. His is the only headstone in Gapuwiak to incorporate a portrait photograph, declaring Bangana's role as a man of 'modern technologies', as he used to describe himself. In turn, Deger recounts how this grave became a favoured site for family portraits, enabling the deceased to be explicitly enfolded in the imaging practices of the living.

Jennifer Deger eloquently traces the strands of dense symbolic significance and the relationships between persons, ancestors and forms of image-making that converge in *Djalkiri #1*, as well as the weight of feeling behind its production. In so doing, she produces an idea of the portrait that, in order to *truly be a portrait* in this context, must enact a whole complex of intergenerational, interspecies and intercultural relationships. By contrast, some photographs of persons, including family photographs, may be regarded as 'simply snapshots'. Only when a photograph is taken up and assembled, activated within a fundamental set of relationships—linking an image of a person to his place, to the ancestors that confer his character, to other qualities of personality as well as authority, to the activities and pleasures for which he is known, to the people who miss him—only then is a picture transformed into a portrait. Thus in Yolngu reckoning we see the accepted face of the portrait flipped—the immediacy of recognition is dismissed in favour of 'the pulsing substrates that extend beyond and beneath the span of a single life'. There are strong resonances between Deger's project and those of Conomos and Weiss, all three transcending accepted parameters of image-making and ways of seeing persons to explore modes of identification that are deeply held, defy fixed or conventional categories, and call out new visual forms of articulation and expression.

Like Maleuvre, Deger foregrounds the idea of the portrait as encounter, invoking the work of philosopher Jean-Luc Nancy. Nancy's writings are particularly pertinent to the interests of all the essays in this collection, as becomes clear in his observation that portraits are a special instance of the wider phenomena of images:

> a portrait touches, or else it is only an identification photo, a descriptive record, not an image. What touches is something that is borne to the surface from out of an intimacy. But here the portrait is only an example. Every image is in some way a 'portrait', not in that it would reproduce the traits of a person, but in that it pulls and

draws ... in that it *extracts* something, an intimacy, a force. And, to extract it, it subtracts or removes it from homogeneity, it distracts it from it, distinguishes it and casts it forth. It throws it in front of us and this throwing, this projection, makes its mark, its very trait and its stigma: its tracing, its lines, its style, its incision, its scar, its signature, all of this at once.[16]

Nancy goes on to elaborate this weight that the image brings to bear upon those who encounter it: the ultimate significance of the image is that it offers up 'a world we enter while remaining before it ... a world, which is to say: an indefinite totality of meaning (and not merely an environment)'.[17]

The essays that follow are all engaged with this power of portraits to draw us into worlds. Their overriding common purpose is to reveal a fundamental symbiosis; to understand the workings of images is to understand something vital of what it is to be human.

---

16   Jean-Luc Nancy, *The ground of the image*, trans. Jeff Fort, New York, Fordham University Press, 2005, p. 4, original emphasis.
17   Nancy, 2005, p. 5.

PART I: The work of the imagination

1

Rembrandt, or the portrait as encounter

Didier Maleuvre

'A good painter', says Leonardo da Vinci, 'is to paint two main things, namely man and the workings of man's mind. The first is easy, the second difficult'.[1] As portraiture came into its own during the Renaissance, it became accepted that a good likeness alone does not make a portrait. The able painter must convey, besides mood and affect, a sense of who the sitter is: their personality and, deeper still, the sense of what it is like to exist as this person. In other words, portraiture is a matter not just of aesthetic proficiency but also of moral and psychological attunement. But how does the painter step into the sitter's subjectivity? How does s/he paint *acknowledgement*? It seems the artist here must depart from the familiar province of *seeming* and enter the unmarked domain of *being*—a puzzling transition if we consider that art traditionally pairs with imagination and make-believe.

In this essay, I argue that imagination isn't an impediment to moral perception. In fact, imaginative depiction plays a crucial role in apprehending others as persons. I develop this line of argument by reflecting on a key feature of portraiture: likeness. Likeness is normally understood to be a property of a person's appearance; but it is also

---

1 Leonardo da Vinci, *Notebooks*, London, Oxford Classics, 1980, p. 168.

clear that, by definition, likeness refers to a model of comparison beyond appearance proper. A person doesn't look like herself—this is a tautology; she looks like the image of herself we mentally draw for her. At first blush a portrait presents the likeness of a person; on consideration this likeness cannot pre-exist the portrait. Thus portraiture is essential to having a likeness, of looking like oneself.

Of interest here is that likeness shifts from the singular to the plural, from the personal to the interpersonal. My likeness relies on another person's creative witnessing. How does the intersubjective nature of likeness inform portrait painting? How, in particular, does the painter represent their commitment to offering the gift of likeness (which is ultimately the gift of personhood) to their sitter? I examine this question through a selective discussion of portrait paintings of Rembrandt, paying special attention to those instances where likeness breaks down for the sake of, paradoxically, preserving the uniqueness of the represented person.

I

It is no use trying to hide the elephant in the room—not an elephant this size. Rembrandt cuts an anachronistic figure in a volume of essays addressing portraiture in the digital age. Next to digital photography, facial-recognition software and web imagery, Rembrandt is bound to look a tad passé. Yet anachronism is far from being the subject of this essay. For nothing about a Rembrandt portrait is out of date; nothing in what I propose to convey about Rembrandt is indifferent to our present circumstances. The time of the portrait, I want to show, is *now*—the now of encounter, the now of the human conversation. And this moment, this now, is the beating heart of great portraiture.

This idea that an excellent portrait radiates personal presence is actually rather uncontroversial outside of academia. Hopefully, the experience I propose to describe isn't foreign to even the gimlet-eyed connoisseur. Wandering through a picture gallery, your eye grazes on seascapes and genre scenes, gods and queens, crucifixions, abductions, rapture and woe, a repentant Magdalene, a defiantly murderous Judith, a congress of happy shepherds. From the corner of your eye you wearily spot a portrait. You lumber up to it. You gaze.

1. REMBRANDT, OR THE PORTRAIT AS ENCOUNTER

Then it happens. Suddenly, or perhaps slowly, but surely unawares, you are drawn into a hypnotic face-to-face. The walls melt away, the shuffling crowd vanishes, the world becomes background and you are alone in the presence, no longer of a picture, but of a face, a person—a person who wants something from you. At last you shake yourself free of the spell. You readjust your gaze: once again it is just a picture you are looking at. And yet it has become much more. The portrait seems to hold the presence, the aura, the heft (there is no right word for it) of a real person. Though it falls short of the real person, in another sense it feels like too much of one. His or her demand on our attention feels unconditional, agonisingly more pressing than the real presences we allow to intrude into our everyday attention. We seem to have had an 'encounter'—a word, and an experience, on which we will want to cast light.

Not that this encounter is unusual. In fact, the subject of Rembrandt's human realism is, rather, a commonplace of art history. But to say that it is commonplace doesn't mean there is anything ordinary about it or that it has been properly looked into. One might even say it has been easier to dismiss, for there is something about the achingly pressing presence of a Rembrandt portrait that outstrips the remit of art historians. It seems to call on the joint counsel of psychologists, philosophers, spiritual teachers and saints. It asks for our reckoning, but reckoning isn't the business of art criticism. Whereas the art critic will often privately admit the bliss of an encounter, professional training, academic discourse and the distinctions of art history journals do not really make room for the language to describe it. Specialised and technical to a fault, the language of criticism is inimical to the 'subjective' haze of encounter.

Rather than emotions and intimations, the professional critic prefers facts, among which, certifiably, is the artefact. Of one thing the learned critic is sure, a painting is a thing. For all its likeness to a person, a portrait is an image, and images don't speak, see or feel. To forget this is to wander off into a magic forest where statues walk and plaster Madonnas weep. But representations are first and foremost facsimiles. However we dig into them we will find pigments and oil and canvas and the imaginary reconstruction of an artist. The hard kernel of reality is out of the picture. Any attempt to recover it is sentimental indulgence; it belongs in the bottom drawer of criticism known as the pathetic fallacy, the mistake of attributing an emotion to the object that evokes it rather than the person who feels it. In sum, if you want a real person, go to a singles' bar, not a museum, and by all means stop trying to have encounters with dry old paint.[2]

In search of scientific facts, art criticism latches onto the social and material context of art. Rembrandt scholars invite us to focus on the conditions of workshop production, the buying and selling of pictures, public taste—indeed any contextual element that helps bury the fact that for three months a human being sat before another, the first to offer their likeness, the second to ponder and recreate it in paint. You may call this portrait a Rembrandt, says the critic, but it is really 'market conditions', 'stylistic conventions' and 'set programmes' that created the paintings.[3] But, of course, this is a will o' the wisp—and most unscientific to boot. Abstractions like 'the market' or 'public taste' do not make pictures. Men and women do. Indeed, to dismiss this plain fact is to commit a pathetic fallacy, and on balance it is probably more scientific to believe in weeping icons than historical abstractions that paint. Of course it is not my intention to lead us to forget that an image isn't what it represents. I am, however, going to look at the person *inside* the portrait to see what lies at the bottom of this naive encounter. Is it a misapprehension? If so, is it pathetic and perverse, or benign and necessary?

II

Some conceptual work is in order if we are to develop the discussion further. In essence, I want to show that looking at a portrait and seeing a face aren't dissimilar actions. To see the face as a person is to see the portrait in it. My hunch is that the realism we naively maintain at the portrait gallery is the same naive realism that allows us to see one another as persons and not things.

---

2   TJ Clark, *The site of death: An experiment in art writing*, New Haven, Yale University Press, 2008; James Elkins, *Pictures and tears: A history of people who have cried in front of paintings*, London, Routledge, 2004.
3   Chief among the anti-psychological school of portrait criticism, see Ernst van de Wetering, 'The multiple functions of Rembrandt's self portraits', in Christopher White and Quentin Buvelot (eds), *Rembrandt by himself*, London, National Gallery, 1999; H-J. Raupp, *Selbstbildnisse und Künstlerporträts von Lucas van Leyden bis Anton Raphael Mengs*, Brunswick, Herzog Anton Ulrich-Museum, 1980.

1. REMBRANDT, OR THE PORTRAIT AS ENCOUNTER

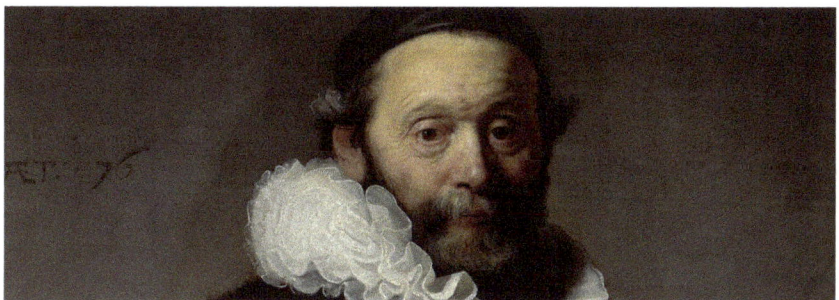

Figure 1.1: *Portrait of Johannes Wtenbogaert* (detail), Rembrandt Harmensz. van Rijn, 1633, 130 x 103 cm.
Source: Rijksmuseum, Amsterdam, public domain images.

A portrait, we are told, is a thing. This is quite true, but empirically speaking a face too is a thing—ridges and dips and holes tied to muscle attachments. It is realist naivety—our sympathetic tendency to project form, intention, sense and feeling—that transforms those ridges and holes into a face. Unless we *imagine* into its surface, unless we take it as manifesting consciousness, a face is a hunk of flesh. Our everyday approach to the human face is, in a restrictive sense, aesthetic: it draws the material data into a portrait, and believes in it.[4]

Infants are precocious portrait-makers when they interpret the blur of eye-mouth-cheek-nose as mother's face.[5] And when young children begin drawing, they start by squiggling faces. Representation starts spontaneously as portraiture. And this isn't because a face is a quaint and interesting circle. Rather children draw a circle because they see a face in it, and drawing it allows them to enact the transfer from mind to mother. We begin our toddler-doodler career as naive realists. We do not depict in order to cover up or look away from human reality but to relate to it through other means. On this score, to insist that a portrait is just a system of paint smears is like the sinister pedantry that would consist in teaching a child to say not 'this is mum', but 'this is a shower of photons bouncing off a face, hitting my optic nerve

---

[4]   On the subject of subjective projection see James Elkins, *The object stares back: On the nature of seeing*, New York, Harvest Books, 1997.

[5]   See John Willats, *Making sense of children's drawings*, Mahwah, New Jersey, Lawrence Elbaurm, 2005; Georges-Henri Luquet, *Children's drawing*, London, Free Association Books, 2001 [1927].

and forming into a mental pattern that denotes another object called mum'. In everyday life we elaborate portraits of each other; we see the face as figuring forth a human being.

This is not to deny that the human brain somehow gets tricked into projecting personality into a two-dimensional facsimile; it is to insist that this sort of emphatic naive projection quickens the normal process of seeing actual faces. My worry is that when critics deny the person in the portrait they undermine the representational thinking that sustains ordinary moral intelligence—the intelligence that allows us to imagine constructively the life of others and behold the face as a portraying-forth. Now this is all very well, but a portrait is a thing, and the face quite another. The former we hang on the wall; the latter we hang not, or else only to punish. But let us look again into the distinction between face and portrait. Our ways of speaking often betray us, and in this instance reveal that the difference isn't a hard-and-fast one.

Of both a portrait and a face we say that they present a likeness. This, we say pointing at a photograph, is a likeness of Winston Churchill, and we thereby designate an object. But we also use the word 'likeness' in another sense; for instance, when we say 'this photograph captures Sir Winston's likeness' or 'Sir Winston and Sir Randolph, his son, share a likeness'. We can also say a likeness binds the young, middle-aged, and elderly Winstons. In these instances we are referring not to an artefact but to an abstraction. This abstraction is no fancy conceit; it is how we identify a person. To recognise Winston Churchill is to check his face against an enduring likeness—a likeness that exists independently of Winston since, as we have seen, Randolph also has a claim to it. Does young Winston look like old Winston, or is it old Winston who looks like his younger self? Randolph looks like Winston, but this is because Winston looks like Randolph. The point is that a likeness doesn't really belong to the person proper. But, then, to whom does it belong?

The observer, of course, and our ability to make a mental portrait out of the living person. All in all, and so far as we recognise one another, we are the artists of each other's likeness. This, we are beginning to see, has an interesting bearing on personal identity. For if identity assumes being identical to oneself, and if such similarity is construed by an observer, then identity will surely involve a strong interpersonal element. It takes at least two persons to look like oneself.

Let's summarise this way: first, a mug becomes a human face insofar as we mentally portray it; second, identity is conditional on recognition; and third, recognition requires the imaginative projection of a portrait onto the face.

III

Let's now carry these abstractions back to the painter's studio. At the heart of Rembrandt's art—I think this is true of all great portrait painters—is an insight into the commonality between being and being depicted; between, if you will, identity and portraiture. The person in the portrait says, 'I am here because I have been seen. I exist because I have been painstakingly acknowledged to exist'. And this statement is no less true *outside* the portrait gallery. There, too, someone's humanising gaze of others is needed to actuate your or my personhood.

The idea that others give us our humanity doesn't sit well with our culture's individualistic ethos. We, the children of Descartes, Locke and Kant, tend to believe in spontaneously autonomous personal identity. Public and private, me and others: this distinction is integral to the modern psyche. The self is a private fiefdom. When the 'I' presents that fiefdom to the world it is always with the sense of putting up a public relations pageant. For the true self is what one deeply is, never what one shows. Hence our propensity to suspect the touch-up job, the slick lie, in portraiture. We cannot help assuming that whatever the intention, a portrait holds a mask over the face. The painter, we say, could only show what the sitter seemed, not who they are.

There are several reasons why this is not true, at least not true of *great* portraiture such as Rembrandt's. Let's begin with the historical reason. The clear-cut duality of private self and public persona, or, if you will, face and portrait, doesn't travel well across the ages. Admittedly the sixteenth and seventeenth centuries did see a trend towards more individualised experience. Castiglione, Montaigne, Cervantes, Shakespeare and Descartes—their works are the milestones of a growing sense of separation between the private self and public life. Until quite recently, however, these were more philosophical exercises than realities. Actual everyday life mostly went on as it had for centuries, woven into an intricately communal web. If Shakespeare did 'invent' the deep modern self, this invention took place on the rowdily public London stage—hardly a solitary affair. Even the proto-individualist Hamlet needs an audience, and a performance of his individuality, to get at who he is privately. He doesn't know himself until he acts out his various social selves. Of course he worries about being honest and true to himself. The problem is that there is no 'himself' until he acts before a public.

This was also Rembrandt's world—a gregariously civic milieu in which very few people would have fretted about the division between their 'true' selves and their social selves. It would scarcely have occurred to them to consider the gaze of others a Trojan horse. Little would they have understood Sartre's Cartesian trepidations about the objectifying glance of others. Seventeenth-century man was an unquestioning public creature. To be and to be seen, to be and to be portrayed wasn't the feuding pair it has become in the modern age of privacy.

If anything, the golden age of Dutch society would have deepened the social embedding of selfhood. Released from feudal vassalage, men and women had to negotiate their lives and livelihoods, their good names and fortunes, in teeming urban environments. Not fixed ancestry but trade and burghers' councils and influence-peddling defined who one was. A drawback of merchant society, aristocrats bemoaned, was that no one was ever relieved of having to prove their worth. No step up the social ladder was secure. The work of garnering social relevance was never finished.[6] Identity was a fungible asset, always in need of recognition and reaffirmation. It was, we might say, permanently on the auction block.

This fragility is the context of Rembrandt's portraiture. It explains the expectant attention of his faces, their susceptibility to slight, their pained need of confirmation. These were the faces of people who lived by the esteem of others. They are the faces of men and women taking part in the strange new experiment of having their portraits painted,

---

6   See Jonathan Israel, *The Dutch Republic: Its rise, greatness, and fall, 1477–1806*, London, Clarendon Press pp. 328–32, 344–53.

a luxury formerly the perk of princes and prelates. Their parents had been commoners, invisible and unpaintable. Suddenly they were sitting in front of a painter's easel, like gawky provincials in Sunday dress—though dress, when it comes to it, was not something you could hide inside because clothes were generally plain and uniform in Calvinist Amsterdam. Sumptuary laws frowned on the wearing of insignia, frippery and showy signs of distinction. One's good name was one's face, bare and uncovered, and this is what Rembrandt looked at, alive to his sitters' expectant mood, which sometimes bespeaks utter vulnerability. The faces he painted look for a witness: for someone with whom they can put themselves in trust.

Very often Rembrandt's portrait commissions were of merchants (the shipbuilder Jan Rijksen, the fur merchant Nicolaes Ruts, the cloth merchant Maerton Looten), men whose livelihoods depended on social exchange and thus on trust, negotiation and reputation (the part of our own self we do not own). Hence the implicit aim of these portraits: to present a face that says to investors, bankers, underwriters and society at large, 'you can trust me', 'your investment is safe with me', 'give me your guilders and I will repay you tenfold'.

Rembrandt discovers, or at any rate chronicles, what happens to the human face in the bourgeois age—the age that made human identity ever so much more fragile, more conditional and more contingent than it had been under the feudal caste system. Under feudalism, in an age of virtually non-existent social mobility, identity was mostly an innate non-negotiable asset, high or low, which fortune, better known as Divine Providence, allocated at birth to the individual. One was born a peasant or a great lord, a *laborator* or a *bellator*, and no amount of striving could turn the former into the latter (not, at any rate, within one lifetime). Enforcing this rigid, one-time allocation of identity was the work of theocratic ideology, which remitted the matter of personhood to divine ordinance, laying bare the contents of one's psyche to God's omniscient and omnipresent eye. Why discuss, debate, argue, doubt or explore the contents of one's soul when all is decreed and defined by the ultimate Judge above? The question of personal identity was, as it were, out of one's hands and, crucially, out of other people's hands as well. Without straying too far into the sociology of the transformation from agrarian feudalism to the mercantile, city-based economy of the nascent modern period, it is well-known that the economic and social experiment first started in the Italian city states of the Renaissance and then more clearly emerged in Flanders, Holland and the cities of the Hanseatic League, together with ordered trade, manufacture and banking, and the political administration of industrial prosperity.[7] With urban mercantilism came social mobility and therefore a more fluid, contingent and change-prone experience of personal identity. No longer was identity a fixed allocation. It was a movable and negotiable asset, a currency subject to the upward and downward re-evaluations of good and bad luck (for this reason the allegoric figure of Fortuna re-emerges during the Renaissance), and subject also to the contingencies of personal success or failure, and consequent civic standing. In sum, identity in the bourgeois economy of incipiently modern Europe had a much more fragile, vulnerable, fungible quality. As society moved from the Court to the Town, identity came to depend on ongoing exchange with equals, competitors, fellow guildsmen, associates, customers, fellow traders and neighbours. Acknowledgement was given, but like all things given could be taken back or refused. We see in the mercantile city just how much identity rested on the currency of one's good name, one's reputation: that is, through the recognition of others.

The contrast between the fixity of pre-bourgeois identity and a contingent bourgeois experience of identity is best seen when we consider the court portraiture of the Cinquecento of a painter like Bronzino against Rembrandt's civic portraiture of mercantile Amsterdam. The high gloss and immaculate finish of a Bronzino portrait, such as the portrait of Eleonora of Toledo, Grand Duchess of Tuscany, conveys but one thing: that the creature before us is a kind of *immaculata conceptio* of identity. Bronzino doesn't delve into the inner springs of personality; he maintains the mystique of aristocratic status, its aloofness, the idea that a great lord is not made but born. The Duchess's subjectivity doesn't wait on our testimony. Nor does it wear on contact or leak. It is decay-proof. Certainly it isn't liable to downward reappraisal. For this reason no grand duchess of Tuscany ever asked a Rembrandt to do her portrait. She who thrives on ignoring the gaze of the awestruck many—this person wants not a Rembrandt but a court artist; the Bronzino of the Medici court or the David of Napoleonic glory, an artist who can rustle up the stainless gloss

---

7   Fernand Braudel, *Civilization and capitalism, 15th–18th century, Vol. 1: The structures of everyday life*, New York, Harper & Row, 1981, esp. pp. 479–525.

of a bulletproof face. Sensitive portraits of tyrants are few because tyrants freeze the person-to-person encounter that begets intimate portraiture: Elizabeth I is a jewel-box, Louis XIV a minotaur, Stalin a poster idol. Court portraiture conveyed all this by holding forth a miracle of synthesis: not a visible brushstroke betrays its making, its workshop provenance.

This contrasts sharply with Dutch portraiture. Unlike its Italianate cousin, a portrait by Rembrandt or Frans Hals doesn't conceal its layered, analytic, obviously manufactured construction. It isn't just that Dutch portraiture doesn't airbrush the corrugations of time and the material genealogy of the individual's flesh. It's that the portraitist flaunts their brushstrokes (thick, streaky, *laboured*), which tell of industry. The strenuous hand admits that these burghers, far from being born into an identity, made themselves who they are. In life as in paint, they are made of contingency.

Social identity in the bourgeois age is work-in-progress. Unlike the Duchess, a Dutch burgher cannot take recognition for granted. Eleonora of Toledo's identity is an awesome fait accompli. The Dutch merchant who sits for his portrait, by contrast, calls on our recognition; his likeness has an expectant, other-directed quality, conveyed by the deliberately tentative, cumulative brushwork. The latter tells us that identity is a mutually constructed thing. Both sitter and painter have to work at it. Identity is interaction, that is, artefact, and it is achingly alive to the confirming look of others. See me, the Rembrandt face says. See me and ponder me, because without you I am not sure. Here identity awaits confirmation. Thus the contrast between aristocratic and bourgeois portraiture, Italian and Dutch, Court and Town comes to this: while a Bronzino *records* a pre-existing face; Rembrandt *recommends* a face to our attention, knowing that this face exists only so far as this recommendation and this attention last.

Where caste and religion prevail, the painter isn't invited to puzzle out the sitter's personality, the facial chiaroscuro of seeing and being seen. The painter doesn't need to plumb the silence of a human face because there *is* no silence. God knows everything, down to the lees of one's mortal soul. This certainty siphons off facial depth and mystery. The faces of the theological-aristocratic age are those of people who know they cannot stop being who they are. If they do pose, their posing comes naturally. One might say that it hides nothing.

First, because nothing is ever hidden (from God); second, because no amount of inner idiosyncrasy, of internal twistedness, can dint the iron of caste identity (a mad king is king nonetheless); and third, because the divide between public and private, the outer and the inner, isn't the antinomy that it would become post-Reformation. This homogeneity of identity helps to explain the mostly flat, hieratic style of portraiture that prevailed until the mercantile revolution of the late fifteenth and sixteenth centuries. Until then a portrait tended to be a symbol, an icon, a cameo, generally cold to psychological probing. It is in the mercantile city-states of Italy, then of Northern Europe that, not coincidentally, portraiture evolves towards a less hieratic style. In the late 1400s, the portrait turns sideways: neither frontal, nor profile, but in-between; half in light, half in shade, a limbo between revelation and mystery. Henceforth, particularly in Rembrandt, when the subject does strike a grand pose it is with a self-undercutting hint of irony; sometimes of parody.

Rembrandt indeed learned from Italianate portraiture, and parodied its forms (Rembrandt sitting himself in the fur and velvet of a Raphael grandee). Art historians regard these portraits as parodic or aspirational—Rembrandt, the son of a country miller and a baker's daughter, either clawing his way into the dream-life of a Florentine prince or mocking its pretensions.[8] Whether aspiration or political lampoon, we cannot for this reason take his self-portraits, at any rate those of the middle period, as straightforward invitations to a one-to-one with the artist. A great deal of window-dressing has gone into them. Less so in the portraits of the late period, when Rembrandt's bourgeois fortune began to turn, and creditors took away his furniture, and his standing among the Amsterdam bourgeoisie began to totter; when, indeed, he became an economic failure. Gone then is the parodic intent, the aesthetic commentary on his Italian predecessors, the insider's joke or political theatre.[9] From then on his self-portraits are more a plea for recognition, that most precious of bourgeois commodities, especially for the bourgeois loser, which, socially speaking, is what Rembrandt became in his last, sad decade. In these self-portraits Rembrandt takes in the full fact of his inner and outer contingency, depicting himself with the same earnestness,

---

8   Mariet Westermann, *Rembrandt*, London, Phaidon, 2000, pp. 153–7.
9   Harry Berger Jr, *Fictions of the pose: Rembrandt against the Italian Renaissance*, Stanford, Stanford University Press, 2000, pp. 427–514.

sensibility and earnest recognition he had given his sitters in the best portraits. Rembrandt is undeniably in dialogue with other painters, in particular with Rubens and the Italians. As such he is in dialogue with art's history, forms and ideas. But his attention isn't merely theoretical, and the subject of his paintings isn't just other paintings. Standing at the easel, Rembrandt is also in dialogue with *people*—his sitters, his relations, his own person, to whom he owes the currency of bourgeois life: that is, acknowledgement, the gift of biography.

The personalism of Rembrandt's portraiture is, first of all, a by-product of a great social experiment: the sea change that was the relative equality of social conditions or, if not equality, at least the breachability of conditions—the fact that social status was now open to new entrants (and also produced outgoing losers). This levelling of human identity (no longer an immutable, God-appointed fixture but a permeable process, an economic variable) is essential to the experience of the portrait-as-encounter. It must be remembered that Dutch painters, whether Rubens, Jan de Bray, Frans Hals, Vermeer, Pieter de Hooch, Gerrit Dou, Jan Steen or Rembrandt, all hailed from the merchant middle class, sometimes from the stratum of artisans and small traders—the same middle class that by and large was the subject of their portraiture. This means that when Rembrandt stood at the easel he did not face princely creatures stratospherically above his own station. He saw fellow beings who competed in the marketplace of social acknowledgement like he did. And like him, the burgomaster sitter wasn't a mythical projection of the grovelling crowd; he was above all a fellow citizen paying another to depict him—that is, to be seen, acknowledged, *portrayed*. This is no simple service, for if the customer's power lies in his fee, the artist holds the spiritual power of recognition. And when it comes to portraying his fellow townsmen and women, Rembrandt doesn't do satire or sentimentality, and he certainly doesn't do adoration. He does civic acknowledgement, which he knows is the mysterious quantity by which he, good bourgeois that he is, lives. So he renders the russet frizz of the man's beard, the sympathetic crow's feet around the eye, the embossing of midlife on the cheek as though each detail were a talisman, the concentrate of an entire life. A person stands forth: not a curiosity, not a facet of everyday life, but a person, a person like oneself, one might say, except that oneself, as Rembrandt acknowledged in his self-portraiture, is far from being an open-and-shut case. It requires *abysmal* attention: literally, a taste for the abyss.

Civic equality (not to mention the Christian equality of souls) enabled the portrait-as-encounter. Which is why, at least to my eye, Rembrandt isn't quite as adept at giving women their full subjectivity. Either lust or a gender barrier or prejudice (we cannot venture to say which) blurs the mirror. He certainly is a better observer of matrons; the younger or more desirable the female, the more he tends to confabulate. It is a creature of fancy Rembrandt paints in the portraits of his beloved Saskia, and for all their hint of intimacy, we feel ourselves being set up to ogle and daydream. Rembrandt is known to paint women in profile, but no man does he ever sit in profile. A profile tends to be much more of a stylised synthesis. In any case it isn't something one has to face. One doesn't have to stare into those eyes. For this reason a profile is easily abducted by abstraction.

Fanciful avoidance also has the better of Rembrandt when he turns to group portraits. The fantastical masquerade that is *The night watch* suggests that he fell for the musketeer mystique. Here he stops looking; he confabulates. We admire the brilliance; address ourselves to the separate person, however, we cannot. Likewise, his pictures of the patriciate of aristocratic young bloods, whom he depicts as soft-focus apparitions, eyes and bodies sidling into some romantic unknown. It is cases like these that, from a position much lower down the social ladder, Rembrandt delivers social mystique as commissioned, with creatures delicately airbrushed out of everyday life. This is Rembrandt at his most Italianate.[10] And for a moment, as with an aristocratic portrait by Titian, we feel the cold whiff of unshakable self-certainty, and of what it is like to exist beneath the notice of people to whom one does not, and could never, matter. The aristocrat of the Baroque courts had his portrait drawn not to solicit public attention but to confirm that all eyes were on him even before he cared to look down. The bourgeois who is Rembrandt's subject secures social acknowledgement *through* the portrait. And social acknowledgement (negotiable, contingent, conditional) is what Rembrandt cannot help distil into his own, especially late, self-portraits.

---

10 On the topic of Rembrandt and Italian art, see Kenneth Clark, *Rembrandt and the Italian Renaissance*, New York, New York University Press, 1966; and Berger, 2000.

1. REMBRANDT, OR THE PORTRAIT AS ENCOUNTER

Compare Titian's *Portrait of a man* and Rembrandt's admiring tribute to the Venetian master, *Self-portrait leaning on a stone sill*. For all Rembrandt's admiration of Titian, he seems not to grasp what makes the latter's portrait so terrifyingly beautiful: its aristocratic disdain. Titian's man doesn't need us to carry on in his magnificent, lip-curled existence. He sees us before we see him, and doesn't find the prospect rewarding. We are an off-glance in his day. Rembrandt's face is another story: it quavers with alertness. Wrinkle-browed, the hint of a bite on his lips, his gaze seared into ours, he is nothing if not determined to catch our eye. He may look dashing under the cocked beret, but the flurried cross-hatching, the crackling frizz of hair, the static bristles of his sleeve all prickle with intent, the lines at dry point crisscrossing his figure in a fever of attention-getting, the strain of which finally tells in the fatigued dimming of his eyes. Or take Raphael's *Portrait of Castiglione* and Rembrandt's homage: Platonic poise and dreaminess on Raphael's side; on Rembrandt's a man who buttonholes our attention lest he cease to exist should we look away. Castiglione exists before and after the portrait; Rembrandt, precariously, *through* the portrait.

IV

The idea that the bourgeois self exists *through* the portrait allows us to revisit another commonplace of portrait criticism. Earlier I betrayed dissatisfaction with some blind spots of materialist criticism. But this isn't to say at all that subjective-emotive art criticism has all the right answers. One of its core assumptions is that a portrait records a pre-existing personality; that it serves as a personal mirror. 'A private dialogue, a lonely old man communicating with himself while he painted', is how one critic explains Rembrandt's late self-portraits.[11] This idea is both obvious and untrue.

First of all, a portrait is much more than a channel of communication; it is an act of creation. A mirror relays a pre-existing likeness, whereas a portrait creates one. Moreover as intimate and personal as a self-portrait may be, it is never a 'private dialogue'. There is little about a portrait that is merely inward or private. Painting is a hands-on activity that generates a concrete artefact. In the work

---

11   Manuel Gasser, *Self-portraits from the fifteenth century to the present day*, New York, Appleton Century, 1963, pp. 90–1.

of art the subjective objectifies itself, and the inner becomes outer. Self-portraiture secretly wants an audience; it asks a public to ratify from the outside who one takes oneself to be on the inside. This way of cultivating external forms throws into doubt the notion of some internally looped personal self.

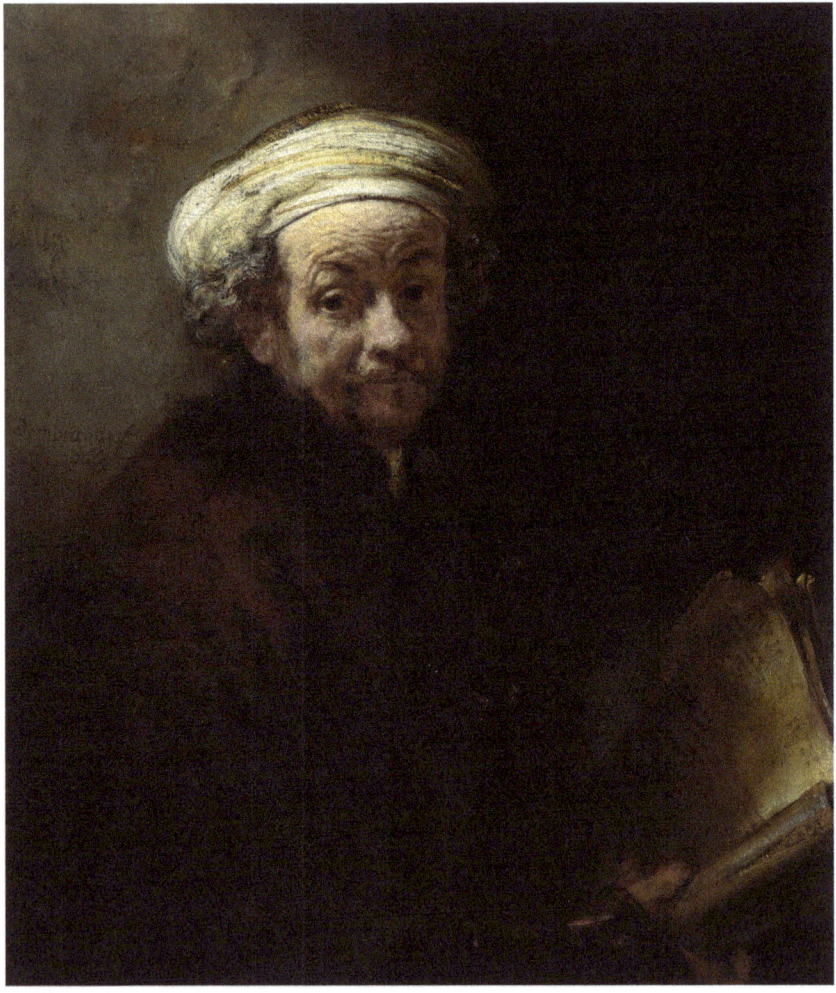

Figure 1.2: *Self-portrait as the Apostle Paul*, Rembrandt Harmensz. van Rijn, 1661, oil on canvas, 91 x 77 cm.
Source: Rijksmuseum, Amsterdam, public domain images.

1. REMBRANDT, OR THE PORTRAIT AS ENCOUNTER

Far from being inward, a self-portrait requires a painter to adopt an external viewpoint. The artist depicts himself not by looking inward but by looking at what other people see. Self-depiction here is filled with the acknowledgement of other people's gaze. It is a confession about the ghostliness of the so-called inner self. Had Rembrandt possessed perfect self-transparency, it is unlikely he would have returned again and again to the mirror over his seventy-eight self-portraits. Rembrandt wasn't himself until he painted himself. And more than a means to construct an identity, self-portraiture was internal to his sense of self. It was just what it felt like to be Rembrandt.[12]

There is a hint of this in his working method. Not for Rembrandt the job of merely capturing his own likeness. The stakes were higher: it was a matter of finding himself. As a pupil described, Rembrandt never began a portrait by contouring or defining his general features but rather by 'violent, flurried strokes ... Painting by means of these strokes, he worked so slowly, and completed his things with a tardiness and toil never equalled by anybody'.[13] Rembrandt didn't 'block' the face and then fill it in. He didn't have a theoretic overview of a likeness; human presence was something he needed to paint his way into, layering and moulding one brushstroke at a time, building towards a climax of recognition that came, or not, at the end of three months, often more, a delay not every Amsterdam patron was willing to endure, which is perhaps why Rembrandt so frequently turned to the long-suffering mirror. Rembrandt worked ad hoc, resisting the easy lure of summarily sizing up the sitter. Hence the iterative paint strokes, the clotted, glutinous, lumpy texture of his surfaces, particularly of the late period. They are of faces travelled through, explored, delved into. Above all, they are incorporate faces, heavy with mortal flesh, with ageing and physicality. We can see the welts of paint laid on, one after the other. We feel the toil, and the duration of making enters the portrait and time becomes one of its dimensions. These searching, overlapping strokes are like a process of approaching; they ask permission for ingress. They are the work of acquaintance. They acknowledge the perfectible, never perfected labour of adjusting

---

12 See Alpers' discussion of Rembrandt portraiture as theatre in Svetlana Alpers, *Rembrandt's enterprise: The studio and the market*, Chicago, Chicago University Press, 1998, pp. 34–6. This analysis supports my intuition that unless it is portrayed, a face remains abstract. But then the aesthetic mode isn't theatre; it makes real people more real.
13 Joachim von Sandrart, Filippo Baldinucci and Arnold Houbraken, *Lives of Rembrandt*, London, Pallas Athene, 2008, p. 23.

to a reality that is more commanding and elusive than painting itself, though it requires painting to come into its own. That reality is the face—civic bourgeois identity in the flesh.

This long, drawn-out painterly labour is a lesson to us whose idea of portraiture is irremediably tainted by photography. Today, in the vast majority of cases, portraiture means snapping a picture. And photography doesn't go much for the soft-footed work of acquaintance. The camera is a hunter, not an interlocutor. It 'catches' or 'captures' a moment. It snaps and snags. Photography is an aesthetic of shoplifting, not of confession. It is also a rhetoric of extreme reduction for it crams the vast and fluid presence that is a human being into a split second snatched out of the air. It purports to trap the human form of life in a quantum. Think of the crushingly vacant eye of Hal 9000, the supercomputer villain in Stanley Kubrick's *2001: A space odyssey*. Here the aesthetic of soul snatching meets the aesthetic of murder. Hal records without seeing, and this is why murder comes so easily to it.

As for the human eye itself, it doesn't see in 1/500th-of-a-second brackets. Cutting into life, a photograph shows what no one actually ever sees. Its nature is forensic, and its use archival. A portrait, for this very reason, it cannot yield since it cannot describe and doesn't wait on a face. It doesn't have the active patience to suffer a reality to emerge. And without the creative patience that is description, without the labour of seeing one's way around the landscape of a face, the human face is but a wan abstraction, a graph, a marker—this independently of how true to life its record may be.

Perceiving the abstract nature of photography depends on whether we remain alive to the danger against which Rembrandt is warning—the danger of distraction. Rembrandt's romance of the face reminds us that our existence hangs on each other's gaze. We are humans thanks to the moral work of mutual depiction. Nothing is so common as to dismiss a face as a thing or a type. Nothing is so tempting as casualness, especially in our photographic, televisual culture, where offhand attention is a style—the 'cool' cat, the slacker who 'chills', the Facebook selfie flashing the orthodontically standardised grin that makes one look like a photograph even before the picture is taken (there is such an undertow of conformity in our scramble for personal recognition).

1. REMBRANDT, OR THE PORTRAIT AS ENCOUNTER

Real portraiture is the opposite of casualness. To portray is an act of looking-at that is also a looking-after. It makes a face matter. It may be informal but it is never casual. And because it is not casual, its products are never generic. A photograph cannot care because a camera lens cannot see what it records. And no matter how great or intelligent or kind a photographer is, he or she cannot force the camera to care. This is why a good portrait photograph is good in spite of being a photograph; it is good by virtue of being lucky—because the button was pushed at the right moment.

Take, for example, the world-famous 1984 photograph of the emerald-eyed Afghan girl also known as the 'Afghan Mona Lisa'. The moniker alone speaks volumes about how little we think of portraiture, or how little we expect of each other. As photography goes it is a striking picture of a strikingly beautiful face framed by a Holbein-green backdrop and a cinnamon headscarf. If the picture is beautiful, however, it is because the girl is beautiful. Photojournalist Steve McCurry was a lucky man with the right equipment. But his skills were of a technical not moral nature. He may well be a big-hearted human being; but the point is big-heartedness is not required to produce a great photo of a face. A photographer doesn't need to be especially attentive, patient, responsive or committed. In principle there is no reason why the 'Afghan Mona Lisa' couldn't be the work of a sociopath. We wouldn't know the difference.

By contrast, imagine a portraitist who is narrow-eyed, cruel, callous, shifty, incurious, absent-minded: their pictures are likely to be caricatures, mangled nightmares—the gropings of soul-blindness. A psychopath can presumably make a good mathematician, perhaps a piano virtuoso, a master of systems; to be a good portraitist it takes an artist who, when at the easel, is morally awake.

Late twentieth-century portraiture is alive to the moral vacancy of photography. Andy Warhol turned out reams of photo-painted portraits that are really an elegy to portraiture: bleached and flattened facial logos that are more trademarks than persons. How quickly has mass-processed photography leached the lifeblood out of a face. Warhol makes portraits of persons who are never truly seen, only recognised—congealed in the formaldehyde of fame, crudely outlined and daubed in the neon glare of instantaneous mass recognition: cognition without encounter. Your face, my face: who has time to notice? The camera lens does it for us. Truly the camera has cheapened the human face, taking the labour (of love) out of it. What took months for Rembrandt to reckon with, the lens shutter dispatches in a trice.

And there is a price to pay for efficiency. The camera's indifference wears hard on the face. There hangs over it the glassy reminder that in between the eye and the sitter there stood a recording device implacably devoid of concern, sociopathically *casual*. Warhol's masochistic charm, we might say, consists in showing what happens to the human face when we allow ourselves to be recorded without being depicted. We revert to flesh, or its postmodern equivalent, plastic (think of Jeff Koon's embalming treatment of Michael Jackson, or Pierre and Gilles' cryogenically candied faces).

Genuinely *depicted* flesh, by contrast, is never just flesh. Rembrandt's famous painting of the flayed ox shows a carcass, which though dead is anything but lifeless. In fact, you might say it isn't dead enough. Whatever we depict as dead is understood to have lost its life. And whatever lacks life is not lifeless. For what lacks spirit by definition ails, is bereft, is soulful—is as throbbingly soulful as that carcass that still screams for the life wrenched out of it. Nothing that is truly depicted is ever lifeless. If meat could not be dead stuff to Rembrandt's eye, then how much less a human face?

The novelist Jean Genet disagrees. He argues that Rembrandt's late self-portraits proclaim a painter who 'had to recognize himself as a man of flesh—of flesh?—rather of meat, of hash, of blood, of tears, of sweat, of shit, of intelligence, of other things too, *ad infinitum*'.[14] Actually this statement disproves itself (at least with respect to blood, tears and sweat). To recognise oneself as meat assumes the power of self-recognition. To be merely meat, to be meat all the way, would take away the ability to see, let alone represent one's self as such. Thus the announcement that one is meat, plastic and shit should be construed as a roundabout refusal to be just that.

Nevertheless, Genet was right in that representation generally wields a leaden touch. The artist peels off a likeness from the living and transfers it to the inanimate canvas, a surface that is as lifeless as the

---

14   Jean Genet, *What remains of a Rembrandt torn into four equal pieces, and flushed down the toilet*, Madras and New York, Hanuman Books, 1988, p. 43.

1. REMBRANDT, OR THE PORTRAIT AS ENCOUNTER

corpse of an anatomy lesson. Perhaps a pause of queasy self-recognition crept upon Rembrandt as he painted surgeons around the dissecting table, in their midst a former person who is now meat, tendons, guts and, yes, paint streaks. Smears and daubs, after all, are what a portrait inescapably *is*. Could this be a clue to the oddest of Rembrandt's self-portraits, the one where he dangles a lifeless heron so that it blocks his face? When torn from the person and nailed on canvas, a likeness is a hunting trophy of sorts. Where, at any rate, is the ontological difference between a painting and a dead bird?

So a portraitist casts the evil eye, and the death-dealing glare is inherent in representation, whether it be the kindergartener's doodle or Ingres' exquisite sketches. Yet in the measure that the artist knows this, so he can also control it. An artist's job is to challenge the confines of his medium, not to plead captivity to its moral shortcomings. The odds are that an image will objectify; this is why there is grace and beauty in the portrait that succeeds in beating the odds.

Rembrandt returned often to the motif of corpses, perhaps because it was an opportunity to reflect on the danger of image-making. Perhaps he understood that portrait painting requires a touch as careful as the surgeon's own, a touch that remedies what even the surgeon cannot. For anatomists bow to the deadening process that runs from subject to object. Surgeons, after all, deal with nuts and bolts, whether they be dead or alive. The painter, by contrast, strives in the opposite direction, from object to subject. And when Rembrandt paints a corpse, it is to affirm its humanity. Such is the case of the stunning *Anatomy of Dr Joan Deijman* (1657), where Rembrandt puts before us an empty chest cavity from which the human heart is intolerably absent. It is the absence we are meant to endure. Call it a reverse portrait, a portrait of the aching absence of subjective life. Here, too, humanity proclaims its own demise, and thereby affirms itself.

This is why, in parting, we return to the portrait that first hypnotised us by its simple plea for solidarity. It is the unguarded confession, the poignant vulnerability of a Rembrandt portrait that moves us. It is the confession that the face in front of us is in need of us; that without us it is not a face but an anatomy. The humanity he or she has is the humanity we give them. The human face truly is tender clay: when we withdraw the feelers of recognition, it goes flat; it dulls, and dies. The portrait lives not by internal combustion but in the same way that the human face comes alive: in the degree to which it is encountered.

Rembrandt took on the work of building the human conversation and this is the work he passes on to us. How we pick it up from here—how long we remain alive to the call of these impossibly soulful eyes—is a gauge of our commitment to the culture of the Town over that of the Court.

2

Pictures for our time and place: Reflections on painting in a digital age

Melinda Hinkson

Social theorist Zygmunt Bauman puts forward the proposition that 'life is a work of art'. The statement appears glib without Bauman's further qualification: 'Being an individual', he suggests, '(that is, being responsible for your choice of life, your choice among choices, and the consequences of the choices you chose) is not *a matter of choice*, but *a decree of fate*'. Identity, Bauman tells us, needs to be created, just as works of art are created.[1] In the present we are, he suggests, all artists of life. Bauman's reflections on the art of identity-making—which point to certain generalised processes at work in our society more than art creation per se—are confirmed in the observations of other social theorists. Arjun Appadurai argues that with the rise of technological mediation imagination is transformed—it 'has broken out of the special expressive space of art, myth, and ritual and has now become a part of the quotidian mental work of ordinary people'; it 'has become a collective social fact'.[2] Sociologist John Thompson writes of the defining ontological challenge that confronts us in the present: to coherently integrate two registers in which we experience others

---

1 Zygmunt Bauman, *The art of life*, Cambridge, Polity Press, 2008, pp. 53–4.
2 Arjun Appadurai, *Modernity at large*, Minneapolis, University of Minnesota Press, 1996, p. 5.

and the world around us—experience we might simply characterise in terms of presence, and the experience of distance that is enabled by technological mediation, in the first instance by the advent of print and generalised print literacy and then progressively by networked computerisation.[3]

Each of these writers is concerned with the way technological mediation brings about a new social landscape in which the onus is on the individual to draw relations of presence and distance into coherent alignment. This 'new' province of subject formation is the 'old' work of artists. As Hans Belting reminds us, the most basic and complex definition of an image is that it makes an absence present.[4] Crucially an image cannot execute its own coming into being. Images are made present by the media that make them tangible and animate them and the bodies that produce and respond to them. Belting's model of image–media–body transcends the presence/absence binary presupposed by the social theorists while continuing to foreground questions of qualitative distinction between differently mediated forms of image. It is a potent model for thinking about relations between persons and images in the present.

In this essay, I briefly consider these issues from the perspective of two quite different locations. The first is the mediated public sphere. The second is the intimate space of painting production. The link between these locations is painting itself, and, more particularly, attitudes to painting, acts of *looking at* paintings and *making* paintings in an era of accelerated technological mediation. Pursuing a nuanced understanding of what might be described as a contemporary cultural attitude to painting, I briefly consider the work of three Canberra-based painters: Micky Allan, Vanessa Barbay and Jude Rae. Significantly, none of these painters is directly engaged with the problem of mediation I have established. All three are committed to painting as a distinctive medium of artistic practice. In looking at their approaches, we nevertheless gain important insights into how technological mediation figures in the cultural practice of painting in the present. We also encounter distinctive

---

3   John Thompson, *The media and modernity: A social theory of the media*, California, Stanford University Press, 1995. A large and complex literature tracks the social consequences of technological mediation from print literacy through to the digital period. Among others see Anthony Giddens, *Modernity and self-identity*, Cambridge, Polity Press, 1991; Walter Ong, *Orality and literacy: The technologizing of the world*, London, Methuen, 1982.
4   Hans Belting, *An anthropology of images: Picture, medium, body*, Princeton, Princeton University Press, 2011.

2. PICTURES FOR OUR TIME AND PLACE

perspectives on the contemporary problematic of imaging identity in general and portraiture in particular. Before turning to consider this work, I want to explore a minor art scandal that erupted in Australia in 2010 to establish a context for thinking about a contemporary cultural attitude to images. Far from being peripheral to the concerns of a book on portraiture in the digital age, I will argue that in tacking between these spaces of looking at and making artworks, we gain insight into the complex interplay between the life history of persons, place and technological mediation that bear upon contemporary creative approaches to imaging identity.

In April 2010, Melbourne artist Sam Leach took out two of Australia's most prestigious art awards—the Archibald Prize for portraiture and the Wynne Prize for Australian Landscape painting. Public outcry followed the revelation that his entry in the Wynne Prize, the painting *Proposal for a Landscaped Cosmos*, was 'a copy' of a work by seventeenth-century Dutch painter Adam Pynacker, held in the Rijksmuseum, Amsterdam. On 14 April 2010, the headline on the front page of *The Australian* screamed 'Double Dutch: Scandal rocks Wynne prize'. Under this headline, the newspaper paired low-resolution images of the two works side-by-side, inviting readers to make their own comparison.

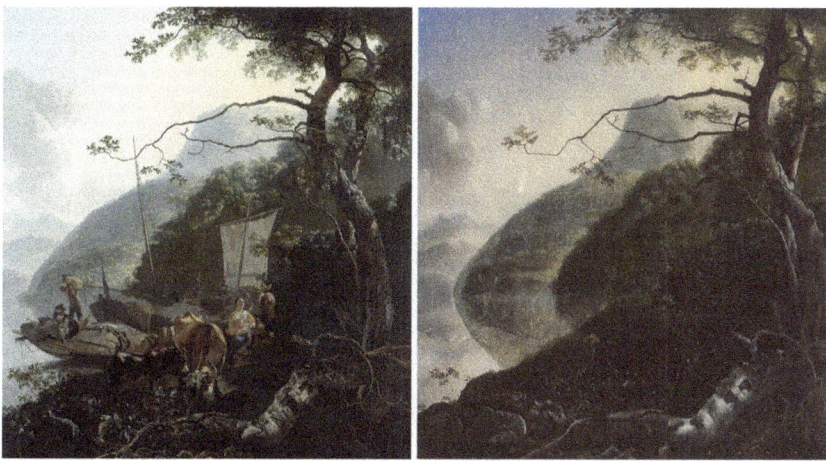

Figure 2.1: Left: *Boatmen moored on a lakeshore*, Adam Pynacker, 1668; Right: *Proposal for landscaped cosmos*, Sam Leach, 2010.

Low resolution scans of these two images were reproduced side by side under the headline, 'Double Dutch: Scandal rocks Wynne painting prize', in *The Australian* and online outlets, 14 April 2010.

Source: Left: Wikimedia commons; Right: courtesy of the artist.

In the days that followed, Australian talkback radio and the blogosphere were alive with commentary on the 'embarrassing' situation. The Art Gallery of NSW was said to be 'a joke'. The judges' insistence that they would have awarded the prize even if they had known the painting was a 'copy' was said to set off the 'old bullshit meter'. The painting was ridiculed not only as a copy but also a 'poor imitation' that one might 'expect to commission in Asia from the … workshops that create these sorts of fakes'. And in perhaps the harshest blow to the artist, his 'mediocrity' should have come as no surprise because, as one commentator revealed, Leach was 'merely a graphic designer'.[5]

Beyond this online chatter, which might be identified as revealing one dimension of a familiar Australian attitude to art, commentary on the Wynne Prize was interesting for what it seemed to reveal about an attitude to *painting*, and more specifically landscape painting. Running through the commentary was a desire to see painting conform to particular expectations. Landscape painting should be unmediated: it should deal with what can be seen; it should be about the 'real' environment. Considerable hostility was directed towards Leach for having depicted a Dutch landscape rather than one that was 'authentically' Australian. While the whole episode might easily be dismissed as a predictable clash between a misguided artist who should have properly attributed his painting and persistent modernist desires among 'the public' for a coherent and knowable subject, I want to suggest that the scandal around Sam Leach's painting can be usefully explored in terms of the interests I have established—particularly for what it reveals about a generalised desire in the present for an authentic art (read: painting) that is independent of the effects of technological mediation and its logic of simulation.

Yves-Alain Bois reminds us that such attitudes to painting and the desire for the integrity of specific media are by no means new and by no means restricted to 'the public'.[6] They emerged in the last quarter of the nineteenth century as part of a general 'attempt to free art from its contamination by the forms of exchange produced

---

5   All quotes are taken from comments posted on Crikey.com, 14 April 2010.
6   See Diarmuid Costello, 'On the very idea of a "specific" medium: Michael Fried and Stanley Cavell on painting and photography as arts', *Critical Inquiry*, no. 34, 2008, pp. 274–312.

by capitalism'.[7] As we approach the present, the urge remains to free art not only from the contaminating effects of the market but from information. Yves-Alain Bois considers the naivety of such longing at a time where 'reproducibility and fetishization have permeated all aspects of life', and indeed have become our '"natural" world'.[8] Given these circumstances, we must shift orientation if we are to identify the substantive work that painting can continue to do. Here Bois invokes Mondrian, for whom painting was,

> a theoretical model that provided concepts and invented procedures that dealt with reality: it is not merely an interpretation of the world, but the plastic manifestation of a certain logic that he found at the root of all the phenomena of life.[9]

It is in this deployment of painting as a distinctive method of working through questions, rather than as a means to an end, that we find a compelling response to glib claims of painting's death in the face of photography and the market.

Two weeks after being awarded the Wynne, Sam Leach made his first public comment, appearing on the Australian Broadcasting Corporation's Radio National, in a 30-minute conversation with senior journalist Monica Attard. For the first time the artist made public his intentions in relation to the painting entered into the Wynne prize, telling Attard, 'I wanted to make a painting that was very optimistic, actually, about humanity'. Leach continued:

> I wanted to make a painting that was going to be about projecting an idealised landscape into the deep future. That was really the point of it; to say ... maybe humans will actually survive, and maybe if we do ... technology could be used to do something that's quite beautiful.

Here Leach revealed that his painting dealt with a technological theme:

> SL: [W]hat I really wanted to do was take that ... idealised, archaic landscape and just flip the meaning from it ... I wanted to take out those things [the figures, the pastoral idyll] the ... golden, idealised past and turn the meaning of the painting into something that's about ... projecting the idea into the future.

---

7   Yves-Alain Bois, *Painting at model*, Cambridge, MIT Press, 1993, p. 235.
8   Bois, 1993, p. 242.
9   Bois, 1993, p. 240.

MA: So then why didn't you just cite the original work?

SL: You know, having said all of that … the original painting itself is not actually what my work is about. My work is about an idealised future … when you put a painting into a gallery basically you've only … got a small amount of information that you can give the viewer and that is the painting itself and the title … I wanted to make sure my title … gave viewers a guide to the painting.

MA: With all due respect, I mean, the title is not what you look at. What takes the eye is the image, and the image is strikingly similar to the Pynacker.

SL: [I]t's clear that the painting is based on that original painting. But actually the content and meaning of the painting is quite different from the original painting. And … *if you … had the original painting and my painting side by side* you'd see that there are a number of distinct differences really.

MA: *I've seen them reproduced in the media*, and to me, what strikes my eye is the jutting landscape … it almost overrules everything else. So again, I'm surprised to hear you say that, in your mind, that you were creating something distinctly new.

SL: [Y]es, the composition is the same. And I did actually work quite hard to maintain the feel of that original Italianate landscape. If you look at the painting and … you think that landscape is like the original 17th century, well, that's really part of the intention of the work. But really, when people look at a painting, *I think many people at least will look at the detail of the painting and think about how that detail informs the entire work.*[10]

This dialogue is revealing for the profound disconnect it registers between painter and journalist, particularly around concepts of representation and authenticity. What I want to highlight is the way each assumes a contrary position regarding the circumstances under which viewers might engage with the paintings in question. The painter makes it clear he assumes a viewer who sympathises with his intentions and, importantly, who will encounter his picture *in all its detail* in material form, scale, technique and texture. He assumes a viewer with an appreciation for paint, not simply as image, but as material dealt with in particular ways. The journalist expresses

---

10 *Sunday profile*, ABC Radio National, Friday 30 April 2010, www.abc.net.au/sundayprofile/stories/2886663.htm, accessed 1 March 2016, emphasis added.

a collective desire for an unmediated painting, but simultaneously assumes the viewer's access to these paintings via rescaled digitised images on television or the internet to be unproblematic.[11] The painter assumes people will be physically *in the company of* his pictures. The journalist assumes the integrity of mediated engagement. Crucially, while the mediated environment is an essential element of this interchange, it goes unremarked upon by both.

Why do I dwell upon this relatively mundane controversy? It raises questions about how we interact with images in a digital age; questions about what kind of work we wish particular kinds of pictures to do for us in the present; as well as WJT Mitchell's question about what pictures may want from us,[12] questions about what is at stake in maintaining qualitative distinctions between different kinds of images. In looking to apply an anthropologist's lens to these questions, I move from the abstract space of public debate to some more intimate positions from which to gauge the interactions between persons and images, shifting register to consider how technological mediation figures in the work of three Canberra-based artists, who describe themselves as painters.

I discovered early on in my conversations with painters that the desire for painting to retain some kind of autonomy from the mediated visual cultural environment is by no means restricted to the abstract world of public opinion. Canberra-based painter Micky Allan recalls the Head of the National Gallery of Victoria Art School, John Brack, telling her years after her 1968 graduation that she should have won the final-year travelling scholarship but that she was ruled out of contention by the judges because she had used a photograph to constitute a subject in her submitted work, rather than painting it direct from life.[13]

As this episode implies, Micky has never harboured a desire to keep painting autonomous from photography. Throughout her career she has moved between and combined several media in her practice. Trained as a painter, painting on canvas is her preferred medium of

---

11 See interview podcast, *Sunday profile*, ABC Radio National, 2 May 2010, www.abc.net.au/radionational/programs/sundayprofile/sam-leach-wynne-prize-winning-artist/3104550, accessed 4 February 2014.
12 WJT Mitchell, *What do pictures want: The lives and loves of images*, Chicago, Chicago University Press, 2005.
13 All biographical material and quotations from here on are from interviews with the author, 1 April and 30 April 2010.

expression, but she has also developed a reputation over the past 30 years for work on etched glass and hand-painted photographs. Micky's biography reflects a common, complex interrelationship between personal experience and creative expression. An early and difficult marriage to another art student saw her painting marginalised in favour of his. By the time the marriage broke down, Micky had stopped painting altogether. Over the next 10 years she lived a highly mobile life, moving between Melbourne, Sydney and Adelaide. While each location gave rise to new artistic projects, canvas painting lay stubbornly dormant.

A move to Sydney in 1978 was precipitated by a personal breakdown. There followed what Micky describes as a 'fabulous period of complete certainty, simplicity, calm'. In Sydney she had her first solo show, which combined drawings, a book of poems and hand-painted photographs, but no paintings.[14] 'I did photographs', recalled Micky, 'because, why, I wanted to paint, but I couldn't do it. It sort of wouldn't flow.' Micky's hand-painted photographs drew considerable interest, but also hostility, in the heady days of photography's attempts to gain recognition as a distinctive form of fine art. Renowned Australian photographer Max Dupain was observed at one of her shows with tears pouring down his cheeks and was heard to declare, 'it should be stamped out!'

But this painter was neither courting controversy nor attempting to make a critical statement regarding the medium of photography. She was drawn to photography by an altogether more personal set of motivations. For Micky, picking up the camera provided an avenue for venturing out into the world, leaving behind the isolation of the studio. Photography, somewhat paradoxically, brought her face to face with other people. 'I wanted that connection and that engagement', she told me, 'even if it was only there in the second of taking the photo.' There were, of course, also qualities of the photographic image that were particularly appealing—'the tonal range you can't get in painting; all that fine grain'. 'And there was something about [this] … this happened, this place exists.' Photography, it seems, as both practice and medium, provided a kind of anchorage, a certainty that Micky needed both socially and artistically. But Micky was repelled

---

14   Micky Allan, *The Live in Show*, exhibition at Ewing and George Paton Gallery, Sydney, 1978.

by the dark room, and especially its chemicals, and was impatient for the photographs 'to be there', ready for her to paint. Photographs were ultimately a form of technical support. Photographs were there in a time when 'painting seemed too hard'.

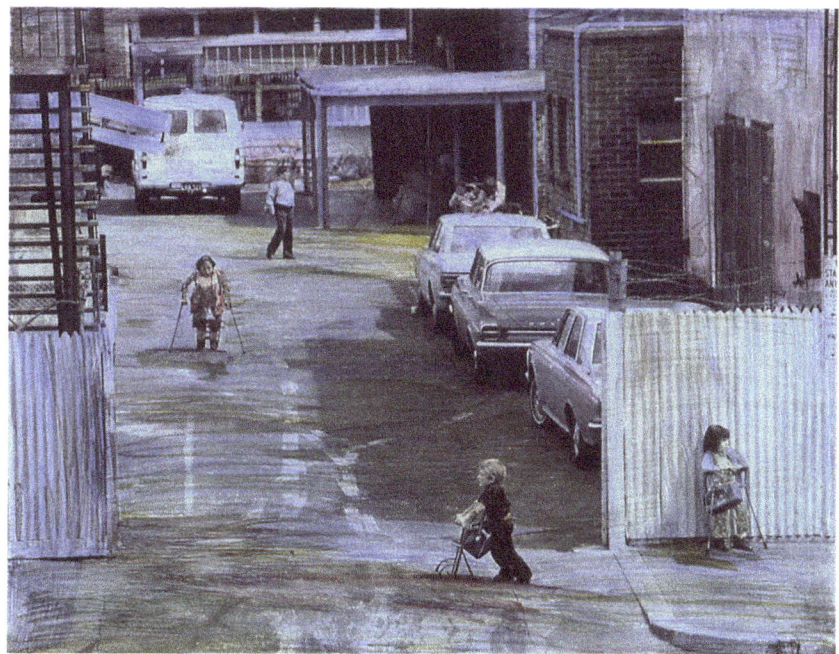

Figure 2.2: *Untitled #2*, from the series *Yooralla at twenty past three*, Micky Allan, 1978, watercolour and coloured pencil on silver gelatin print, 27.7 x 35.2 cm.
Source: Courtesy of the artist.

Then followed a conscious decision to 'give up the photography', a challenge as difficult, one might surmise from her way of speaking about it, as giving up booze or cigarettes. Going cold turkey, Micky took herself, along with some travelling companions, to the red centre and camped out for an extended period near Uluru, the iconic heart of Australia. Without a tent and living on meagre rations of potatoes for days on end, Micky and her friends wandered around exploring the landscape during the day and then basking in the 'velvet, embracing, expanse of the night sky'. Like a well-disciplined patient withdrawing from her addiction, Micky did not photograph, paint or draw during this time, although she did make some sketches from the window of the moving car. On her return to Adelaide, the creative urge was back and

Micky produced large charcoal drawings of what she remembered of the desert landforms and 'these imagined strange insects'. She refers to these drawings as some of her favourite pieces. 'They really surprised me, what came out ... They were going into that totally imaginative area that is responding to the place.'

Through the 1990s to the present, Micky has produced series upon series of painted work, wrestling with how to figure in paint the complex interaction of the infinite in the everyday, the interplay between material and immaterial experience, the rhythms of nature, crisis and renewal, and echoes between deep sea, night sky and outer realms of the universe. Mesmerising sweeps of paint are in some works interrupted by a raised fractal, a scatter of glitter, cut coloured-glass marbles, highly textured painted strips. These motifs—often depicting entities beyond tangible reach, such as deep-sea creatures and space matter—are regularly constituted with the help of photography and scanning equipment. The photographic images feed Micky's imagination in ways that are critical to her practice.

The energy and conflicting pulls of Micky's imagination are as evident on the walls of her studio as they are in her manner of speaking. When I visit her one day in April 2010 I am taken aback. In place of the usual riotous scene of colour, materials and works competing for her attention, is an austere calm of empty bench tops and blank white walls. Canvases are stacked away, turned so that their backs face into the room. Materials are filed in draws. The studio has been transformed into a blank canvas awaiting its tenant's next move. As I take a seat a flash of blue catches my eye—a pile of underwater photographs from a recent trip to Cape Leveque in Western Australia lies on a table next to Micky's laptop, tickling her interest.

Jude Rae, who painted Micky's portrait (Figure 2.3), speaks about the studio as lab.[15] But in her case it might also be characterised as a critical theory workshop. Her paintings are consciously constructed meditations on the nature of contemporary perception. Yet they are emptied of any obvious content that might draw the viewer's attention to such perceptual processes. Jude's still-lifes are of bottles, cheap vases, plastic containers. Her main aim, as she describes it to me, is 'to neutralise the force of association that those sort[s] of

---

15   Henceforth all quotations are from interviews with the author, 12 April and 23 April 2010.

objects [still-life objects] carry with them'. She wants to reinvigorate a supposedly exhausted genre via a new set of questions. This process gained further dramatic force with Jude's second series of still-lifes: of fire extinguishers and gas bottles, produced in the wake of 9/11 and the second Gulf War. Her subsequent series of portraits of people with their eyes closed, and then of people engaged in looking at things beyond the reach of the viewer, are similarly a form of genre critique. A particularly striking painting, *Self-portrait (the year my husband left)*, which won the 2008 Portia Geach Memorial Award for portraiture, poses further questions regarding mediation and concealment and the complex encounter of painter and viewer in the work itself.

Jude works with a deep awareness of painting's *lack* of autonomy; particularly how the forms of vision brought to bear on and through paint today are deeply entwined with the wider visual cultural environment. She wants to produce pictures that get us thinking about how we look at things under these conditions. In order to do so, she needs to withdraw from the 'visual chaos' and into her studio, which she characterises as 'like an extension of my psyche'. Here Jude closes the curtains and immerses herself under fluorescent light in the work of painting, with or without the semi-controlled intrusion of the outside world via Radio National playing in the background.

Some months before our conversations in her studio, Jude was asked to produce a nude for an exhibition being mounted by her New Zealand dealer.[16] She was eager to be involved but when she came to confront the task encountered a number of hurdles. The first was the genre itself and its historical baggage. As she put it to me: 'How do you make a painting of a nude without a mythological framework?' The second was confronted in the doing. Jude found that she fell back onto the method of the life class, where, to quote her, 'you just plonk a person in front of you and you paint them'. In this case, the person had to be plonked naked in Jude's studio, which was a very challenging experience. The model turned out to be 'too present' to enable the imaginative process to kick in.

---

16   *Naked*, on show at Andrew Jensen Gallery, Auckland, 29 April–16 July 2010.

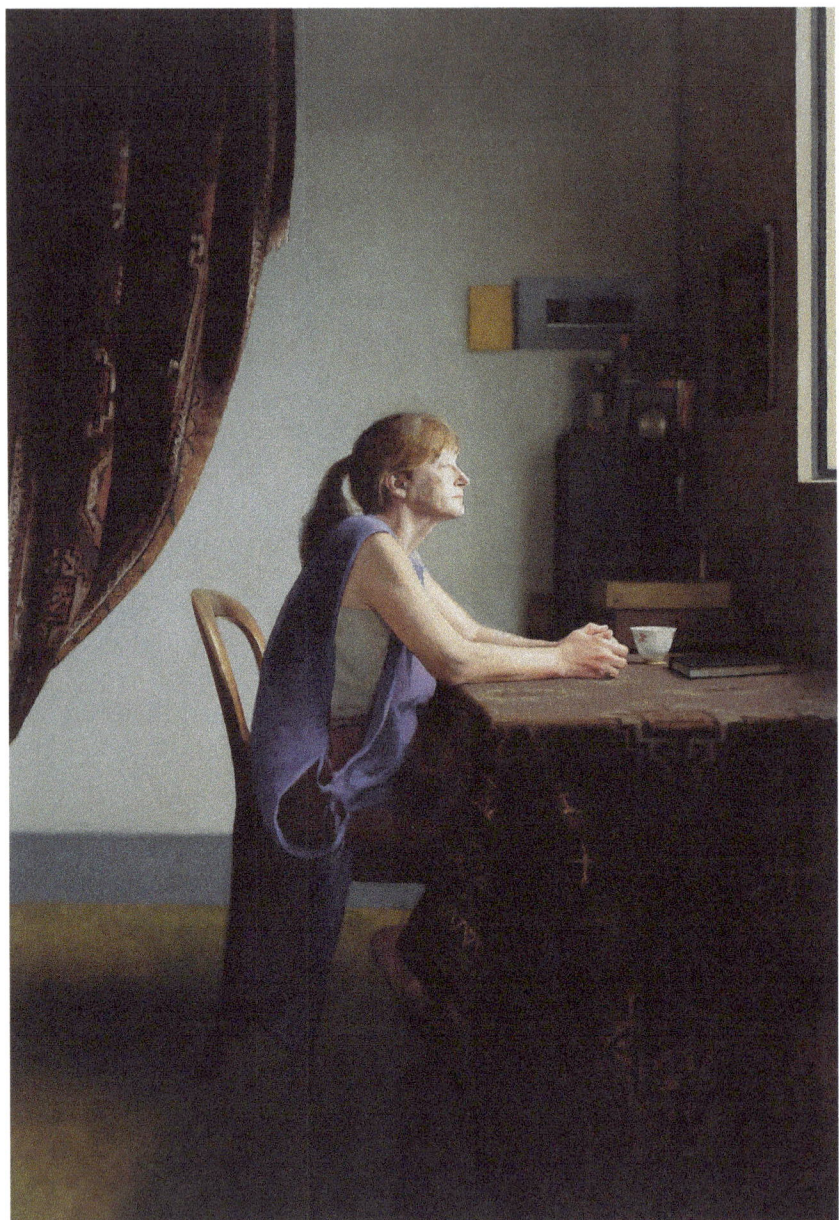

Figure 2.3: *Large interior 173 (Micky)*, Jude Rae, 2005, oil on linen, 180 x 120 cm, winner of the 2005 Portia Geach Memorial Award for portraiture.
Source: Courtesy of the artist.

One day, out of frustration, Jude brought her old Canon camera into the studio and set it up to take some video footage of herself while she danced around naked, striking poses to get a sense of the light, trying to work out how she might use a model in that particular space. From this footage she produced a series of blurred, highly pixilated still images. Looking through them Jude saw not pictures of herself but signs that were graspable in terms of art-historical precedent—one particular image stood out, its qualities seemed to reference paintings by Degas, as well as an ancient sculpture of a boy taking a thorn from his foot.

So what had happened in this process? For Jude the camera became a necessary and highly productive distancing mechanism, an objectifying mechanism. As Belting would have it, this doubly digitised process produced a medium for an image, and in so doing enabled the production of a subject—herself—to which she would not otherwise have had access. The photographic process allowed Jude to distance herself from her own body and the problems of the genre, as well as getting 'around the issue of the model in the studio'. In this seemingly simple, stripped-back charcoal drawing on paper is a paradox enabled by the camera.

Jude's drawing (Figure 2.4) is made by a painter who is consciously aware of the effects of the camera on painting—its 'lack of distortion', 'lack of the problems of drawing', its 'hardness and harshness'. While artists like Gerhardt Richter make paintings that comment directly on the visual possibilities and constraints of photography,[17] Jude's engagement with the medium is more ambivalent. She told me she had a problem with photography intervening in painting 'for a very long time'. 'The guilt that somehow if you use photographs you're somehow cheating the world is still very powerful.' What liberated her was recognising that 'vision is governed by expectation … When you experience that, it's like, what is the difference between working from a photograph and working from a set of expectations?'[18]

---

17   See Peter Osborne, 'Painting negation: Gerhardt Richter's negatives', *October*, no. 62, 1992, pp. 102–13; also Paul Rabinow, *Marking time: On the anthropology of the contemporary*, Princeton and Oxford, Princeton University Press, 2008, p. 116.
18   Rabinow, 2008, p. 116.

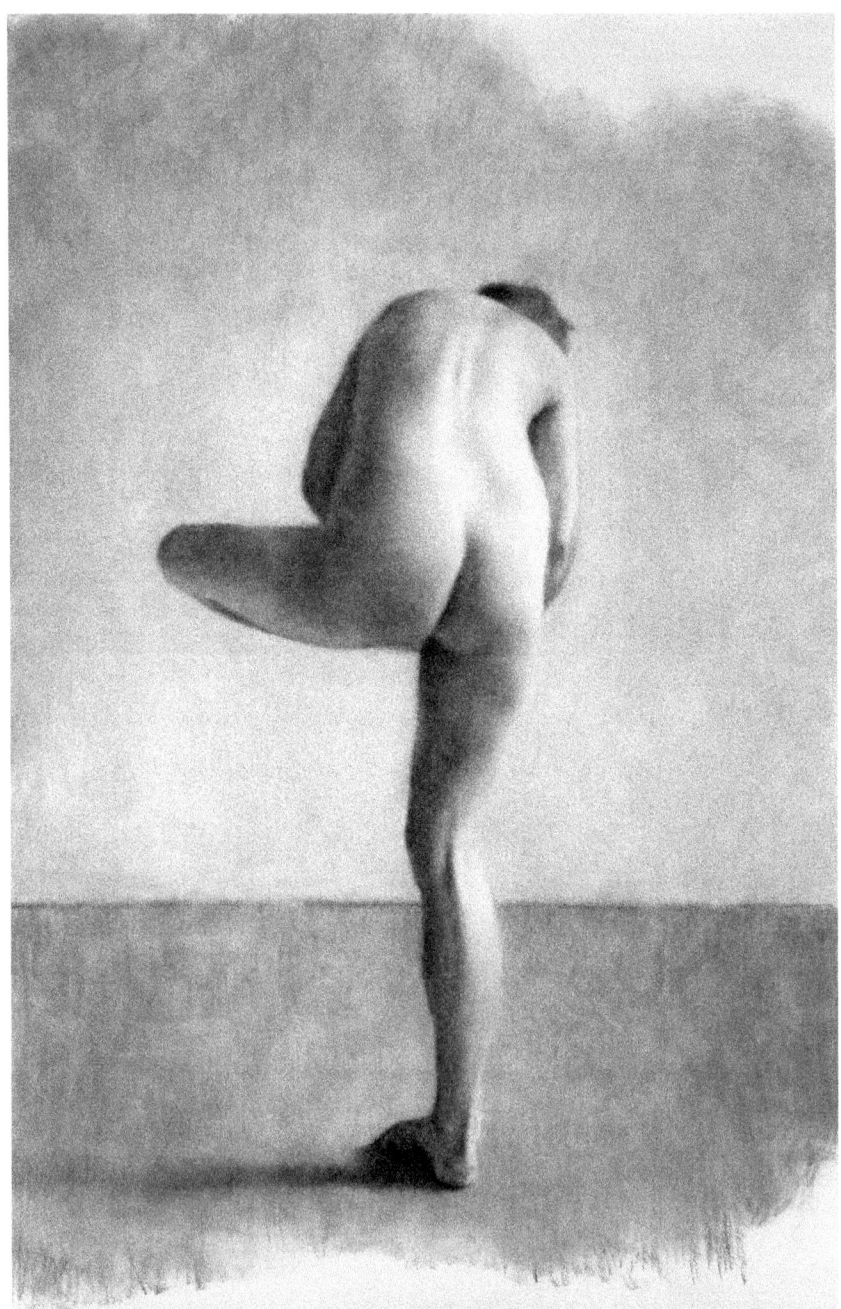

Figure 2.4: *Drawing 101 (naked)*, Jude Rae, 2010, willow charcoal on Fabriano paper, 220 x 140 cm.

Source: Courtesy of the artist.

In the case of the nude project, the pixilated photograph worked as a trigger for the imagination precisely because it was unlike other photographs, which tend to give 'too much information'. Because a photograph presents an absent subject, Jude reflected, it is 'much less overwhelming in all sorts of ways than having the model in front of you … It … creates a space of imagination. It doesn't close it all down …' 'Working from a photograph', Jude tells me, '… my mind will … often … allow me to reflect in a more dreamlike way on my experience of that person. Which is not possible when they are here in front of me. It can take me quite a long way.' So here we are presented with one kind of instance of the beauty of distance. In slightly different ways both Micky and Jude's use of photography seems to share with Gerhardt Richter a desire to counter (or at least temper) the subjectivist tendencies of painting.[19] Their use of technological mediation is undertaken in support of a thoroughly contemporary culture of painting, not to suggest its end.

A third painter, Vanessa Barbay, confronts the abstract mediation of our time with a poetics of a different register.[20] Vanessa describes herself as trying to 'discover ways of painting animals that express, or at least incorporate in part, a "regime of involvement" as differentiated from that of scientific detachment'. The regime of involvement invoked is starkly devoid of sentimentality. Indeed, Vanessa seeks to transcend the abstract modes of engagement and representation through which such emotions might be carried. She collapses any clear distinction between representation and the real by incorporating into the pictures themselves pigment and material drawn directly from her subjects— dead animals, road kill—and their environments. From a distance, a painting appears as a mottled swirl of dark and lighter shades of brown, an apparent experiment with colour and materiality. Up close, the surprising essence of the work is revealed: echidna spikes jut out from the canvas at 90 degrees, matted hair and sedimented flesh hold the composition in place. 'Echidna and rabbit-skin glue on canvas', as the materials list for Vanessa's *Sorcery painting (autumn echidna)* (Figure 2.5) makes clear: the animal *is* the painting. In this sense, the pictures Vanessa makes are not representations in any conventionally understood sense of the term. These transformational pictures re-enact

---
19   As observed by Rabinow, 2008, p. 116.
20   This section of the essay draws from Melinda Hinkson, 'Vanessa Barbay: Painting our animal selves', *Art Monthly Australia*, no. 259, 2013, p. 88.

and meditate upon something of the human–animal relations that have led to the loss of life of the particular subject with which each work is concerned. Specificity is crucial: place and the materials of particular places loom large in the choices Vanessa makes in the production of each work.

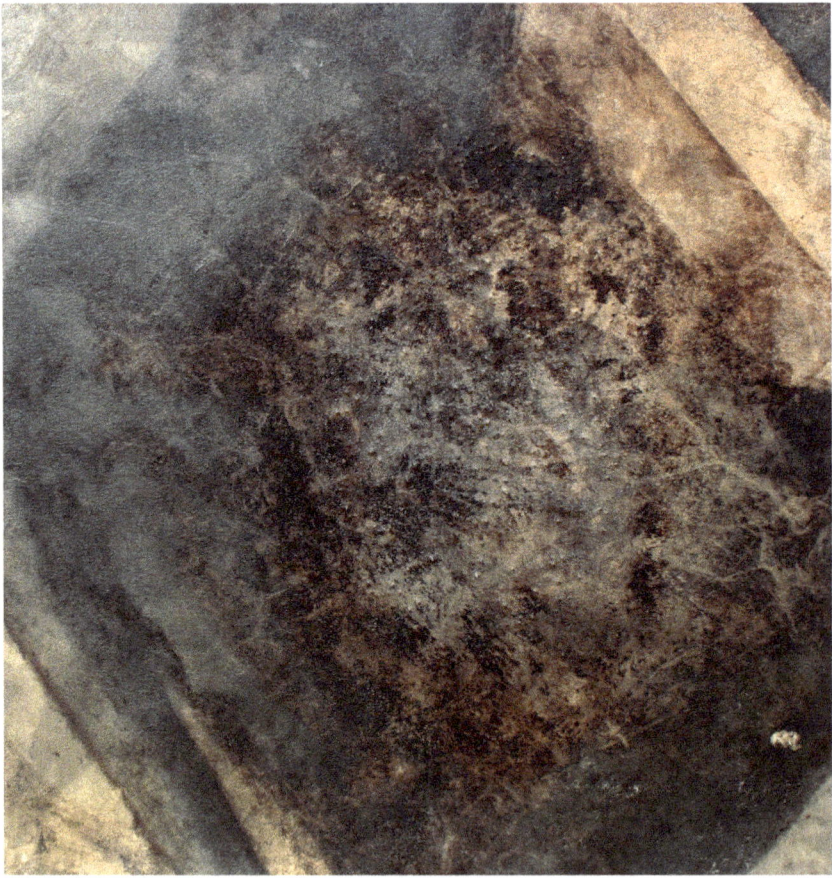

Figure 2.5: *Sorcery painting (autumn echidna)*, Vanessa Barbay, 2011, echidna and rabbit-skin glue on canvas, 84 x 80 cm.
Source: Courtesy of the artist.

Vanessa describes her method as a kind of mortuary practice, one that enables her to collaborate with the deceased animals, to make works that are redemptive acts, transcending the objectification that lies at the heart of classical painting. Her practice involves a carefully managed decomposition process. Dead creatures are placed on canvas, laid out on a sprung bed base and left to the elements beneath a eucalyptus tree on a Monaro property. After a period of months, the canvases acquire shroud-like impressions of bodies, bits of putrefied flesh, as well as eucalyptus sap, dust, rain, marks left by other animals and faint grid-like impressions of the wire mesh protecting the corpses from predators. Most (but not all) shrouds are then domesticated/ deodorised, being steeped in vinegar and infusions of eucalyptus leaves to leach the odour of decomposing flesh.

As Vanessa considers what further creative involvement each shroud asks of her, she gives attention to the particular and local circumstances of each creature's demise. Her choices are also shaped by a wider critical interest in cross-cultural attitudes to the non-human universe, and by an eye attuned to the sacred offerings of nature. *Gift (autumn rosella)*, an ethereal silhouette of a rosella in flight, is the ultimate mystical outcome of the decomposition process, untouched by Vanessa's painting hand except for a coat of rabbit-skin glue. This magical picture has the aura of an ancient religious painting.

Other works are outcomes of the delicate balance between Vanessa's painterly imperative—as the daughter of a taxidermist/collector and two generations of Hungarian artists she has inherited a deeply felt obligation, 'the need to replicate what I see around me'—and her aspiration to transcend that imperative. Where she takes up the paintbrush she does so with a light touch. Wider influences of a childhood closely lived among animals dead and alive, and in association with the Koori community at Vincentia on the NSW South Coast, are evident. Vanessa's more recent research with Kunwinjku painters in Arnhem Land also leaves traces—in the repeated use of *delek*, spiritually charged white pigment; in restrained experiments with cross-hatching; and in her pervasive attention to the possible sacred outcomes of collaborative engagements between humans, other species and the environment. If Vanessa's artworks are portraits, they demand a reinterpretation of that genre for these works foreground an inextricable set of relationships between the deceased subjects of her paintings, the environment in which those subjects lived and died, and the human attitudes implicated in their demise.

While Vanessa's approach to painting enacts a critique of the abstraction that characterises the dominant contemporary attitude to nature, this does not amount to a rejection of technologised methods.

Many of Vanessa's works have been created with the intervention of a computer, scanner or projector. The projected outline of a bird's nest and dead bird are traced with gesso onto canvas prepared with nothing but rabbit-skin glue. The completed work enfolds the projected image as a component of its making, but, like Jude's nude, does not reveal its crucial involvement to the viewer.

To some extent these technical supports are drawn into the process of making paintings under the pressure of the institutional environment in which they are made—the university-based art school.[21] Vanessa's strong moral preference to paint directly from life (or death) is qualified by her concern to meet the requirements of her PhD program, to reveal the processes of making to her examiners, and to meet the 'milestones' and projected outcomes of annual plans. In this respect, her carefully crafted regime of involvement with her subjects and her practice are challenged by the institutional requirement to make paintings more quickly than might otherwise be the case. Projecting images of dark and light onto the canvas so that they might be traced out with efficiency is one kind of compromise made by painters in the art school setting, alongside other constraints related to the cost, and therefore choice of materials, size of canvases and number of paintings made.

* * *

To link the consideration of these painters' work back to the issues with which I began, in describing our vision of the world as 'bifocal', anthropologist John Durham Peters suggests that one of the great ironies of contemporary experience is that the distant, or the global, which we grasp through media images,

> becomes clear through representation, whereas the immediate is subject to the fragmenting effects of our limited experience. Our sense organs, having evolved over the ages to capture immediate experience of the local, find themselves cheated of their prey.[22]

---

21 See the contributions to Brad Buckley and John Conomos, *Rethinking the contemporary art school*, Nova Scotia, The Press of Nova Scotia College of Arts and Design, 2009, for an examination of the range of issues and pressures brought to bear on university-based art schools in the present.
22 John Durham Peters, 'Seeing bifocally: Media, place, culture', in Akhil Gupta and James Ferguson (eds), *Culture, power, place: Explorations in critical anthropology*, Durham and London, Duke, 1997, p. 79.

John Durham Peters seems here to capture something of Jude Rae's experience of being overwhelmed by the presence of the naked model in her studio. We may well observe that studio-based nude life-painting was a common mode of painterly practice of an earlier period. In the digital era, the physically present model may no longer be a familiar or regular element in painterly practice, as painters take inspiration from all manner of objects and phenomena, mediated in all manner of ways. In what Mitchell describes as the latest biocybernetic turn in our relationship with images, the image-worlds created in our time enact the increasingly central and intimate place of technologies in a distinctive way of being human.[23] The subjectivity of persons who identify as painters is as much caught up in these transformations as is the case for the rest of us.

Yet, as a number of writers have observed, paintings continue to demand a different register and temporality of engagement from the fleeting, screen-based images that currently dominate daily experience. TJ Clark and Didier Maleuvre argue that, increasingly, we take the attitude that characterises our interactions with fleeting commodified images into our engagements with other kinds of images, including paintings.[24] This is the logical consequence of late capitalism, which has called out not only a distinctive form of image but, along with it, a distinctive cultural attitude through which persons interact with those images.

It is unsurprising that under these circumstances there may be a strong social demand for painting to stand for what is thought to be natural, or unmediated. While the painting practices considered here demonstrate that painting in the present is technologically mediated activity, these artists continue to privilege what they understand as a *logic of painting*; that is, a method of working-through, a method that only at its conclusion gives rise to 'production'. What is strikingly the case across the work of these three painters is that none wish painting to be free of the possible effects of technological mediation. Their enterprise presupposes a *flow across* art forms and ways of seeing: the possibility of troubling, and indeed *undermining*, binary

---

23   Mitchell, 2005.
24   TJ Clark, *The sight of death*, New Haven and London, Yale University Press, 2006; Didier Maleuvre, 'A plea for silence: Putting art back into the art museum', in Hugh Genoways (ed.), *Museum philosophy for the twenty-first century*, Lanham, MD, Alta Mira Press, 2006.

distinctions such as those between presence and distance, immediacy and abstraction, materiality and intangibility. Given this, there is a kind of double movement in their works—on the one hand, a drawing of attention to thoroughly contemporary phenomena, on the other, a casting of their concerns in more transcendental, universal terms.

In this way, painting practice might be grasped as a form of myth-making. During my discussions with painters I have been regularly reminded of anthropologist Claude Levi-Strauss' work on myth, which he describes in terms of a universal human need to enact in narrative form the contradictions with which we live.[25] Within the structures of myth, Levi-Strauss identifies elements directed at overcoming those contradictions. Art, he suggests, lies midway between science and myth. Artists construct objects from a limited set of materials and tools, but the objects produced are simultaneously objects of knowledge. Artworks have a special ambiguity in that they are both closed *and* open forms.[26] This kind of interpretation is particularly helpful for thinking about the distinctive place of painting in our digitally dominated contemporary world; painting is both *of* the times and *contrary* to it. Painting may be observed to stand outside of and be opposed to the digital yet, as we have seen, its practice often unfolds in intimate engagement with digital technologies, in much the same ways that painters work within and against the temporal structures and ways of seeing associated with the digital visual culture environment they inhabit.[27] Contemporary painting carries its charge in how it holds this apparent paradox in productive tension. As a medium of the present, painting cannot simply be described in terms of the materials that render its finished form.

The works of these three painters indicate a dilemma that returns us to the Sam Leach case. Viewers of Jude Rae's nude or Vanessa Barbay's animal shrouds or Micky Allan's underwater worlds have no access to the stories and techniques of how these pictures were created. And unlike Leach's painting, their titles give nothing away. Thus I conclude by posing several questions. Does it matter that a charcoal

---

25   Claude Levi-Strauss, *Structural anthropology*, volume 1, Harmondsworth, Penguin Books, 1977.
26   Claude Levi-Strauss, 'The science of the concrete', *The savage mind*, Chicago, Chicago University Press, 1966.
27   See Melinda Hinkson, 'Australia's Bill Henson scandal: Notes on the new cultural attitude to images', *Visual Studies*, vol. 24, no. 3, pp. 202–13.

drawing would not exist but for a technologically mediated process of creation? What difference does it make that a painting is composed of the very materiality of its subject? The answer returns the weight of responsibility to the viewer. Just like the journalist interviewing Sam Leach, the viewer of these paintings may not hear or see the message the artist is attempting to convey. It is only when we slow down to look[28] and allow pictures to work on us that they establish themselves as images that speak to us and to our contemporary visual culture environment. In Jude Rae's work, we have a nude that refuses to give up its face and front the gaze of the viewer, a nude that refuses to present itself in the visual language that most commonly addresses the late-capitalist consumer. The work of each of the three painters considered here refuses to conform to conventional expectations of what painting is for. Or are these simply beautiful pictures? You be the judge.

Acknowledgements

Ethnographic research with Micky Allan, Vanessa Barbay and Jude Rae was conducted in 2010. I am most grateful to each of these artists for welcoming me into their studios and for their openness and critical engagement in reflecting upon what it means to be a painter in the digital age.

---

28   As Maleuvre, 2006, appeals to us to do.

3
Diasporic looking: Portraiture, diaspora and subjectivity

Gali Weiss

How does an understanding of diaspora contribute to the way we think about and respond to the world around us? For a number of scholars, diaspora is one of the most relevant social formations for framing the way we understand our times. Some even propose that diaspora is the only social formation that enables cultural identity to survive in a globalised world, describing 'diasporised' identity as one that can hold together seemingly contradictory positions.[1] Diaspora discourse and theorisation offer a critical space for thinking about the mass movements of people that defined the twentieth century and continue to shape the twenty-first.[2] More significantly for this essay, that space is also one in which we can explore how diasporic experience influences the way we view, articulate and aestheticise ourselves and the contemporary world.

---

1   In relation to contradictory positions of identity, Daniel Boyarin and Jonathan Boyarin write of 'an Egyptian Arab who happens to be Jewish, and a Jew who happens to be an Egyptian Arab'. Relating to gender, they argue that 'rather than the dualism of gendered bodies and universal souls ... — the dualism that the Western tradition offers—we can substitute ... bodies that are sometimes gendered and sometimes not. It is this idea that we are calling diasporized identity'. See Daniel Boyarin and Jonathan Boyarin, 'Diaspora: Generation and the ground of Jewish diaspora', in Jana Evans Braziel and Anita Mannur (eds), *Theorizing diaspora*, London, Blackwell Publishing, 2003, p. 109.
2   Braziel and Mannur, 2003, p. 3.

Representations of 'face', fluidity of gesture and form, notions of presence and absence, self and other, the real and the imagined; such themes, which relate to conceptual, philosophical and material expressions of 'being', have always been part of my art-making. It was only as I embarked on practice-based academic research that I identified this practice in terms of portraiture. Simultaneously, I came to understand the significance of diasporic experience for my artistic vision, a vision emerging from a family history of migration, closely held cultural and spiritual values, and identification as Israeli-Australian. While the idea of diaspora has evolved and changed considerably in recent decades,[3] what continues to be recognised as common to all diasporic communities is an emotional allegiance to the 'old homeland'. Most critical attempts at characterising diaspora refer, whether explicitly or by implication, to a centre or home of origin—historic, current or imaginary.[4] The connection to a home other than where one is situated, and thereby the promise or possibility of a return or quest for a return of sorts, lies at the heart of diasporic consciousness. Diasporic identity at once belongs and does not belong to both the home of origin and the adopted home. Diasporic consciousness involves a sense of difference and multiplicity of belonging, a sense of 'otherness', and hence of displacement. The identity of the displaced is not 'complete' as a distinct, fixed identity but, in the words of Zygmunt Bauman, is 'wholly or in part "out of place" everywhere, not ... completely anywhere ... nowhere will one be fully "at home"'.[5] Diaspora can in itself, however, be viewed as a particular space of belonging, in which, as Stuart Hall claims, 'diaspora identities are constantly producing and reproducing themselves anew, through transformations and difference'.[6] For Hall, the future existence of diaspora identity is in its continual re-creativity, re-being; that is,

---

3   According to Braziel and Mannur, theories of diaspora 'have emerged in area studies, ethnic studies, and cultural studies as a major site of contestation. Since the journal *Diaspora: A Journal of Transnational Studies* was inaugurated in 1991, debates over the theoretical, cultural, and historical resonances of the term have proliferated in academic journals devoted to ethnic, national, and (trans)national concerns'. See Braziel and Mannur, 'Nation, migration, globalization: Points of contention in diaspora studies', in Braziel and Mannur, 2003, p. 2.
4   Robin Cohen, *Global diasporas: An introduction*, London, University College London Press, 1997, p. 2.
5   Zygmunt Bauman, *Identity: Conversations with Benedetto Vecchi*, Cambridge, Polity Press, 2004, pp. 13–14.
6   Stuart Hall, 'Cultural identity and diaspora', in Braziel and Mannur, 2003, p. 244.

in its' 'becoming'. It is with these ideas, this particular conjunction of absence and presence, of belonging and not belonging, that I wrestle in making portraits, and which I explore in this essay.

Diaspora as a way of viewing the world

Diaspora—*the* diaspora as I knew it—was a familiar term that referred specifically to the extensive history of the Jewish people. Until only a few decades ago, diaspora was likely to refer to the dispersion of Jews from their original homeland over 2,000 years ago; although sometimes also to the centuries-old dispersion of Armenians from their original and then fragmented homeland. Since the late 1960s, dispersed communities once described as exile groups, overseas communities, ethnic and racial minorities and so on have been re-identified in the terms of diaspora.[7] The complexity of diaspora is evident not only in the range of definitions that are currently in circulation but in the variety of diaspora now identified and the variables within each of these.

My family history demonstrates this: my parents were part of the Jewish diaspora in Eastern Europe in their respective countries of birth before 'returning' to their biblical homeland in Israel, at that time Palestine. When I was a child my parents migrated again, this time with family, to Australia, where we were active in the Jewish community and identified as Israelis living in Australia. As a young adult I returned to live in Israel, then returned after 14 years to live again in Australia. This history of attachment to Israel is so embedded in my family identification that I once heard my Australian-born daughter, when asked by a new acquaintance where she 'came from', answer, 'Israel'. My family has continuously moved backwards and forwards between places, real and imaginary, experiencing the paradox 'of and between location and dislocation' that is a common dimension of diasporic positioning.[8]

---

7   Khachig Tölölyan, 'Rethinking diaspora(s): Stateless power in the transnational moment', *Diaspora*, vol. 5, no. 1, 1996, p. 3.
8   Avtar Brah, *Cartographies of diaspora: Contesting identities*, London and New York, Routledge, 1996, p. 204.

Avtar Brah proposes a viewing of diaspora through a 'politics of identification' as opposed to a 'politics of identity', accommodating the different identities people inhabit that interweave relations of race, gender, class and sexuality.[9] If we accept an idea of diaspora that goes beyond definitions of particular minorities, then how are notions of diaspora placed and enacted within creative production? How do we use the 'language' of diaspora and its inherent ambiguities to both 'read' and depict notions of identity?

Diaspora, and particularly the profusion of diaspora and diasporic identity in the past few decades, has affected both metaphorically and materially the way in which we understand notions of identity, individualism, boundaries and so forth. With this in mind, we can speak of the role of artistic practice not so much in terms of reflecting who we are but as a performative mode of agency that engages us in a positioning or negotiating of a form of subjectivity.

Ernst van Alphen claims that art can act as agency for cultural discourse; it has the power to transform the ways in which cultural issues are conceptualised, as well as represented.[10] Art practice not only reflects culture and philosophy, it provides us with a way of understanding, such that art can be viewed as 'a mode of thinking'.[11] We can see, then, that both diaspora and art can be viewed as frames for undertaking cultural studies and philosophy, not only as historical products.

As already noted, what is constant within diasporic consciousness is the existence of a relationship with a homeland and thereby a continuity of belonging or reference. It is this relationship, this inescapable link to a history, that is at work in my approach to portraiture. More precisely, my practice is driven by an urge to maintain some form of connection, imaginary or actual, with a past (of the genre—that is, its history—and of the portrait's reference) while exploring new meanings and possible futures.

---

9   Brah, 1996, p. 93.
10   Ernst van Alphen, *Art in mind: How contemporary images shape thought*, Chicago, University of Chicago Press, 2005, p. xiii.
11   van Alphen, 2005, p. xv.

As I explore below, crafting notions of identity and representation through diasporic consciousness opens a distinctive way of viewing and experiencing art. In the case of the contemporary portrait, such a view is attentive to the ambiguities inherent in both diaspora and portraiture: the tensions between stillness and fluidity, stability and movement, belonging and displacement, difference and sameness, presence and absence, being one and multiple.

Diasporic visual culture

Through the final decades of the twentieth century, the visual arts were being 'disentangled' from their traditional forms such as painting and sculpture and repositioned not only within fine arts but within a broader visual culture, thus foregrounding a new discourse on the nature of contemporary visuality itself.[12] Diasporic visual culture is an area emerging within visual culture studies, giving special focus to the visual representation of diasporic experience and identity. Nicholas Mirzoeff recognises the paradoxes involved in attempting to represent diaspora, since by its nature contemporary diaspora cannot be fully known, seen or quantified: 'A diaspora ... cannot be represented from the viewpoint of one-point perspective.'[13] The space of diaspora exists in multiple times and places, encompassing those who leave as well as those who stay and those who return. It is multiple, fluid, and at times paradoxical. It is about the future as well as the past. While diasporic identity can be understood in terms of 'double consciousness' as a tension in belonging, or as Mirzoeff claims, as a dialectic between past and present, it may also be rethought in terms of an indeterminate future to come.[14]

Just as concepts and terms of identity are continuously evolving, so too are the terms of portraiture. Portraiture in western art is a genre whose credibility in art-historical terms traditionally depended on notions of authenticity. The conventions of portraiture claim referentiality as the element that differentiates the portrait from all other artistic genres.[15]

---

12   Barbara Kirshenblatt-Gimblett and Jonathan Karp (eds), *The art of being Jewish in modern times*, Philadelphia, University of Pennsylvania Press, 2008, p. 1.
13   Nicholas Mirzoeff (ed.), *Diaspora and visual culture: Representing Africans and Jews*, London and New York, Routledge, 2000, p. 2.
14   Mirzoeff, 2000, p. 4.
15   Richard Brilliant, *Portraiture*, Cambridge, MA, Harvard University Press, 1991, pp. 7–8.

Informing the traditional portrait is its indexical relationship to a particular individual outside the picture. Contemporary discussions of the terms of portraiture, however, range from echoing these older ways of thinking to new conceptualisations that challenge the genre's conventions of presence and authenticity.

Visualising the copy as a tool for new thinking

Susan Buck-Morss has argued that what is powerful in a photograph or digital image is not its ability to re-present but its ability to generate meaning. As previously suggested, the authenticity of the image as art-object may matter in terms of art history (as the product or reflection of a historical period or person), but within visual studies the reproduction takes on meaning in new ways beyond the idea of origin: 'The image disconnects from the idea of being a reproduction of an authentic original, and becomes something else.'[16] Buck-Morss calls reproduced images, specifically as produced by digital technology, 'tools of thought' that mediate between things and thinking.[17]

Perhaps this is the approach taken by Hélène Cixous when she writes of Roni Horn's photographic portraits: 'These are not photographs, these are portraits of looks that don't allow themselves to be taken, snapshots of instants, series of winks of an eye.'[18] Horn's photographic portraits, despite the repeated imagery of the individual photographed, do not represent that individual, claims Cixous. In her *Portrait of an image 2005: Isabelle Huppert impersonating herself in her film*,[19] the viewing position is a face-to-face engagement with the image of a face. As the title implies, the artist's intention does not seem to be to depict the 'real' Isabelle Huppert. Cixous explains how this series challenges the referential purpose of the portrait:

---

16   Susan Buck-Morss, 'Visual studies and global imagination', *Papers of Surrealism*, Issue 2, Summer, 1991, p. 23.
17   Buck-Morss, 1991, p. 20.
18   Hélène Cixous, 'A kind of you: 6 portraits by Roni Horn', catalogue, ACCA, Melbourne, 2007, p. 8 (from her 'Portraits of portraits: The very day/light of Roni Horn', in Cixous, *Poetry in painting: Writings on contemporary arts and aesthetics*, ed. Marta Segarra and Joana Masó, Edinburgh, Edinburgh University Press).
19   Cixous, 2007, p. 64. For an image of this portrait in part, see www.hauserwirth.com/artists/images-clips-view//?artist_id=14&a=roni-horn&p=66, accessed 2 January 2014.

[it] deconstructs the entire traditional unthinking approach to the thing called Portrait, the use made of the word Portrait, when it is referred to people. For this to happen the Portrait must personify the image. The difference between an image and a face: the face sees you. The image does not see you. Is seen. The gaze of the Portraitist gives a figure to the image.[20]

The image alone is not the portrait, and the person the image relates to provides only a fragment of the subject. As Didier Maleuvre argues in this volume, it is the artist's gaze that creates the possibility of the image becoming a face, which as a consequence engages the viewer so that they might discover the 'pearl' that is the portrait. The portrait is a matter of relationality.

The image, the copy

Can a photograph, or reproduction, in itself provide evidence of the 'realness' of an original? The digital age has shown us that the filmed or photographic image can be manipulated, that virtual images can be created, referring not to a real existence outside the image but to the *idea* of a reality.

How can authenticity remain a value in a medium that centres on reproduction, especially when reproduced images are copied, repeated and layered? It would appear that continued reproducibility distances the viewer from an origin and thereby creates a sense of loss of truth, truth being a notion often aligned with origin.

The use of repetition has been central in the work of Chinese-Australian artist Lindy Lee—from her 1980s works using photocopied Renaissance portraits, to her current work in which she draws directly on personal history and family ancestry. Many of Lee's works from the 1990s incorporate repeated images of photocopies of European Old Master portraits into grid or linear formations, playing with differing degrees of visibility and variations in colour tone. This work was informed by Lee's consciousness of her diasporic identity, using the copy as a metaphor for 'unbelonging' or cultural displacement. Lee was

---

20   I have reproduced this and subsequent quotes from Cixous as they appeared in the ACCA catalogue 'A kind of you: 6 portraits by Roni Horn', with the understanding that the visual representation of the text, including grammatical omissions, are congruent with Cixous' meaning. Cixous, 2007, pp. 12–13.

born in Australia of Chinese heritage. She has stated, 'I had always felt a fraud—a copy, and a flawed one at that ... I was counterfeit white and a counterfeit Chinese'.[21]

In *An ocean of bright clouds, an ocean of solemn clouds* (1995) (Figure 3.1), Lee uses 25 photocopies of a single image in varying degrees of exposure so that the face in the work appears and disappears in tone and form but is decipherable through repetition. Significantly, the repetition of the face does not enhance its visibility or particularity, but rather reduces it to anonymity. Rather than a portrait of a fully present individual, Lee creates a heightened sense of the tension between presence and absence.

Melissa Chiu points out that in adopting the copy as a methodology, Lee is attempting to locate herself within the western art-historical canon, at the same time as disrupting that tradition by transforming the notion of the original into the anonymous and reproducible. Lee's use of repetition in the different versions of the original on each panel is not structured as a progression or narrative but as an entity. Here repetition is used to suggest how identity differs according to time and context in 'a state characterised by moments of flux and uncertainty'.[22]

Edward Colless suggests that viewing Lee's 1990s portraits from the position of cultural tradition has the effect of casting Australian culture as a version or 'copy' of European culture. Colless views these portraits, which simultaneously obscure and delineate the face, as metaphors for displaced cultural memory:

> These plaintive ghosts from an Old World hang forever at both a temporal and geographical distance from us. Looking at Lee's appropriated portraits we lose and partially recover images from the past, but images of a cultural tradition that was never really our own. Perhaps we are condemned to see them this way—those original works of art—as remote and speechless icons, because we are their false descendants. Just as the artist considers herself a false descendant of European art, producing false copies of that art as her own.[23]

---

21 Melissa Chiu, 'Struggling in the ocean of Yes and No', in Benjamin Genocchio and Melissa Chiu, *Lindy Lee*, Sydney, Craftsman House, 2001, p. 16.
22 Chiu, 2001, p. 16.
23 Edward Colless, 'Lindy Lee: The many faces of Lindy Lee', *Artcollector*, Issue 26, October, 2003, www.artcollector.net.au/LindyLeeTheManyFacesofLindyLee, accessed 2 January 2014.

3. DIASPORIC LOOKING

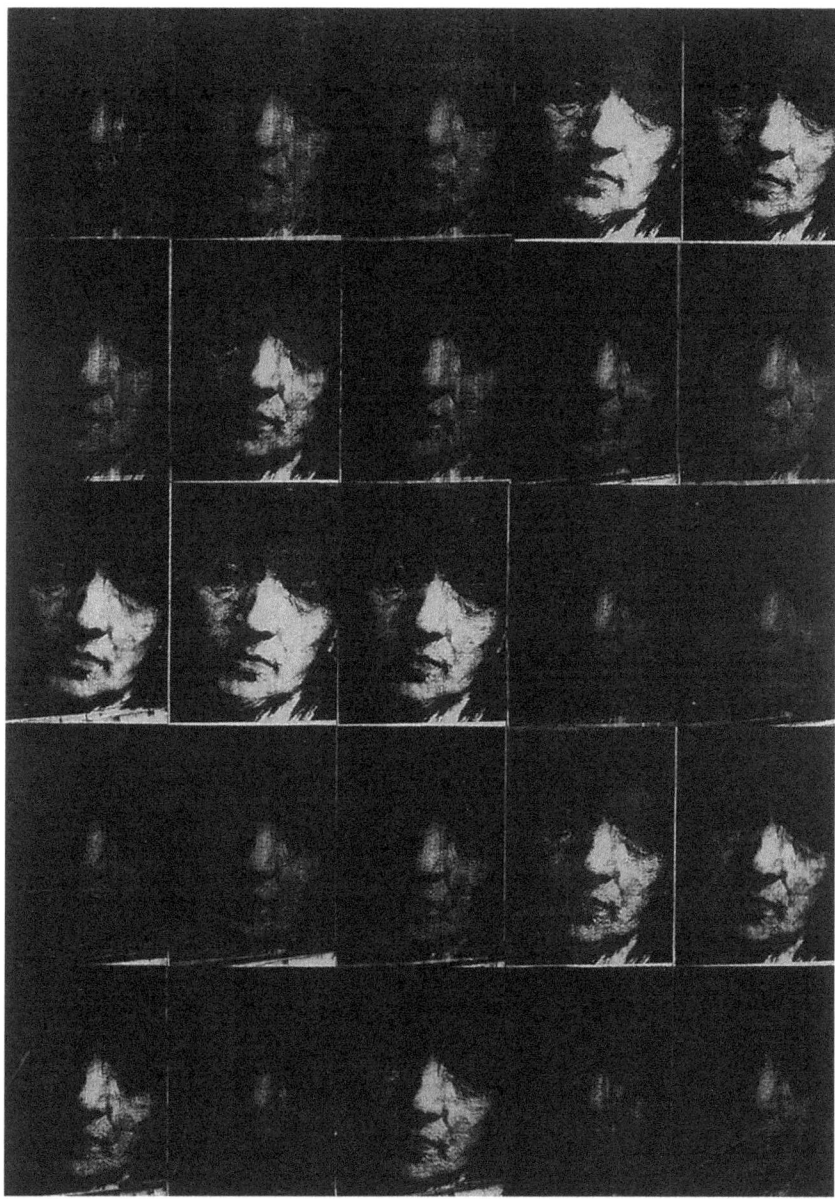

Figure 3.1: *An ocean of bright clouds, an ocean of solemn clouds*, Lindy Lee, 1995, photocopy and acrylic on board, 205 x 143 cm.
Source: Courtesy of the artist and Roslyn Oxley9 Gallery, Sydney.

IMAGING IDENTITY

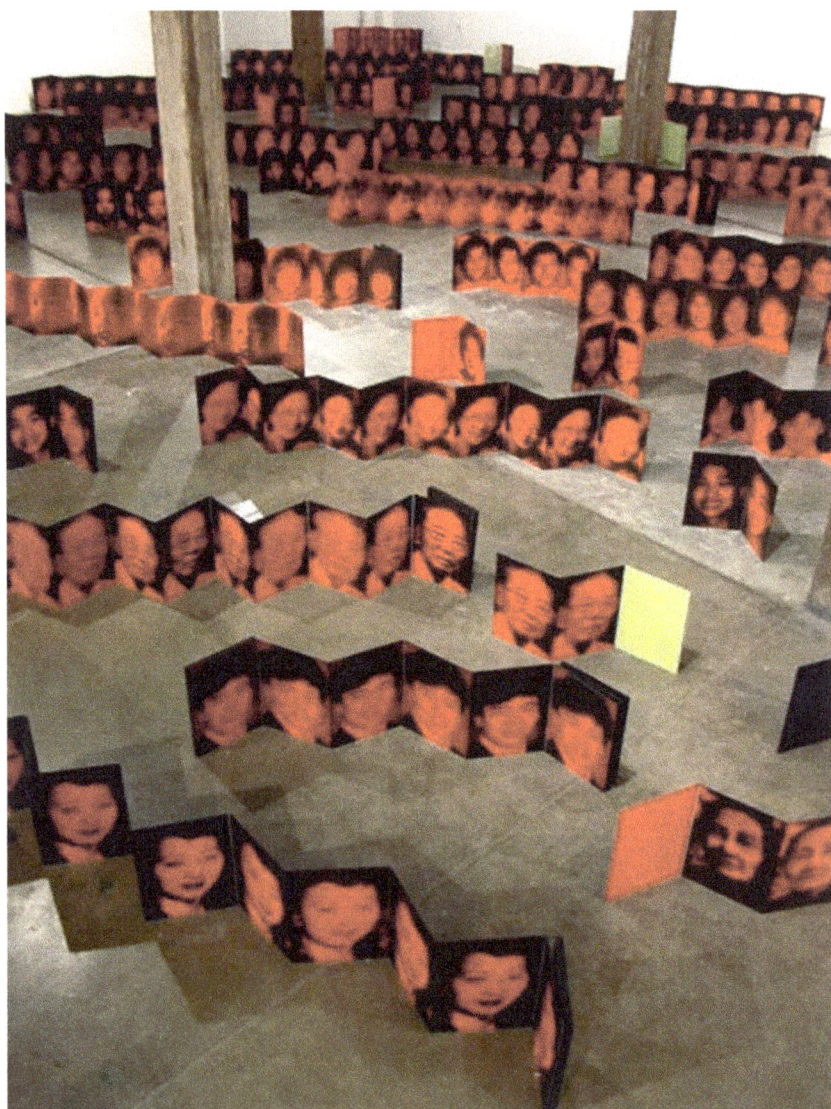

Figure 3.2: *Birth & death*, Lindy Lee, 2003, Installation Artspace, Sydney, inkjet print and acrylic on Chinese accordion books, installation dimensions variable.

Source: Courtesy of the artist and Roslyn Oxley9 Gallery, Sydney.

A copy, however, as Colless notes, can only be regarded as 'false' or 'bad' when it is compared to the original. Lee's art produces a new sense of original by deviating from what it has copied while nevertheless relating to that original as the basis of its being. While these works could be claimed to be self-portraits of sorts, relating to cultural memory and artistic ancestry, Lee has in recent years turned to more direct forms of personal history and family ancestry.[24]

Her 2003 installation *Birth & death*[25] (Figure 3.2) comprises one hundred concertina books of eighteen panels of family-album images of enlarged faces that journey across the floor of the gallery space. The gallery becomes inhabited with Lee's Chinese family, past and present, alive and deceased, in stillness and in movement. The installation is at once a collective portrait and a self-portrait, a family genealogy and a moment in time.

Familial looks and postmemory

Family photographs are likewise central to Marianne Hirsch's study of *postmemory*. Postmemory, explains Hirsch, is a particular way of relating to the past through imaginative investment and creation. It 'characterises the experiences of those who grow up dominated by narratives that preceded their birth, whose own belated stories are evacuated by the stories of the previous generation shaped by traumatic events that can be neither understood nor recreated'.[26] The photograph, in particular the family-album photograph, whose images and narratives extend well into subsequent generations, facilitates this transference. Such a photograph can be read as trace; the trace of the photographed person or place; an 'outline' trace of their materiality; and as the trace of a time that no longer exists. This photograph signifies both life and death, for it shows evidence of the object that was photographed and at the same time we recognise the sense of the 'having-been-there' that creates a sense of loss in the viewing.[27] This photograph both blocks memory, because it is not reviving experience, and attests to its past reality.[28] The function of the photograph as postmemory is as a site that mediates between past and present.

---

24 Colless, 2003.
25 Roslyn Oxley9 Gallery, *Lindy Lee—Birth & death—Roslyn Oxley9 Gallery*, 2013, www.roslynoxley9.com.au/artists/20/Lindy_Lee/471/38857/, accessed 2 January 2014.
26 Marianne Hirsch, *Family frames: Photography, narrative and postmemory*, Cambridge, MA, Harvard University Press, 1997, p. 22.
27 Hirsch, 1997, p. 20.
28 Hirsch, 1997, p. 82.

Hirsch has developed the notion of postmemory in relation to Holocaust survivors, but considers it useful in describing the process at work in the continuity of collective memory in diasporic situations. The idea that memory has both public and private dimensions is integral to the diasporic vision, for this dual status shapes and marks it. This shared memory forms the basis of the traditions and practices of diasporic communities, and the basis of their existence. Without the shared memory of the home of origin and of a collective if diverse past, even if mythologised or abstract, diaspora would not exist. According to Hirsch, the inheritance of history as postmemory distinguishes it from memory as recollection, 'by generational distance, and from history by deep personal connection'. Photographs can connect first- and second-generation remembrance, memory and postmemory, for they represent what has been and what no longer is, but also what continues to be from the position of those who do the viewing.[29]

What is particularly meaningful in family photographs is the performative function of the 'affiliative' gaze, a term that Hirsch uses to argue that there is a particular kind of viewing identification in relation to the familial image:

> Recognizing an image as *familial* elicits ... a specific kind of readerly or spectatorial look, an *affiliative look* through which we are sutured into the image and through which we adopt the image into our own familial narrative. Akin to Barthes's move from the studium to the punctum, it is idiosyncratic, untheorizable: it is what moves us because of our memories and our histories, and because of the ways in which we structure our own sense of particularity.[30]

The affiliative look is not a gaze that is restricted to 'knowledge' of or about the subject but one in which identification follows the particular intimacy of a familial look or exchange of looks. The affiliative look is characterised by its collective sense of intimacy and familiarity. It is the search for this kind of intimate *acknowledgement of experience* rather than *recognition of identity* that guides the artistic choices I make in producing portraits.

---

29 Hirsch, 1997, pp. 22–3.
30 Hirsch, 1997, p. 93.

3. DIASPORIC LOOKING

The practice of portrayal

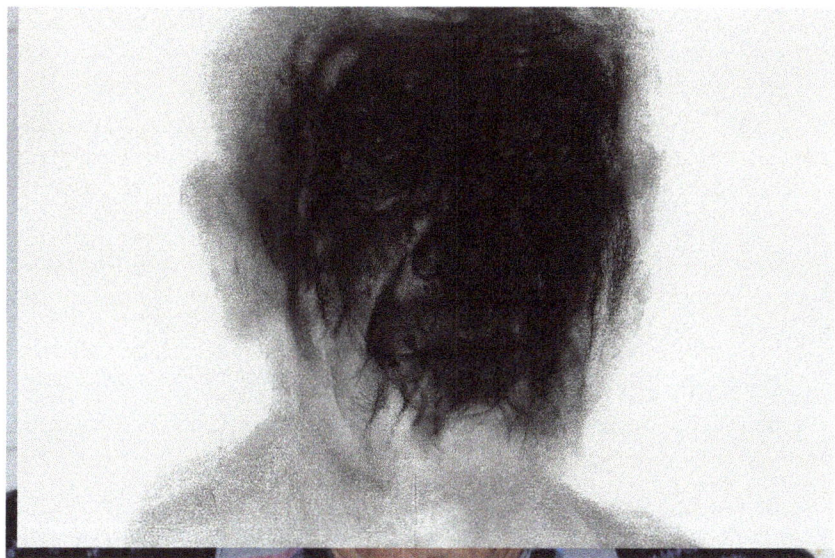

Figure 3.3: *Aaron*, Gali Weiss, 2000, solvent transfer, charcoal, graphite, 76 x 56.5 cm.
Source: Courtesy of the artist.

I had been questioning the function of the portrait in my art practice for a number of years, though it is hard to pinpoint the precise time the problematic nature of portraiture first arose for me. Was it with the depictions of my father in the series *Aaron* (2000) (Figure 3.3)? One of my main concerns then was how to depict the expanse of my father's lifetime in a single image. The more I drew his face at each sitting, and the more details I placed on the paper, the more insignificant the details became. My layered charcoal applications were in effect erasing underlying details, yet I could not stop revisiting those details for they seemed to me in constant change. I decided to 'ground' the image by using a photograph to convey his image stilled, in play with the action of drawing. When I reviewed these images it made sense to me that the viewer's first impression of *Aaron* was not to be a clear one; though reference to the particular man remained recognisable, details of his features were presented ambiguously. The portrait series of Aaron became one of multiple and fluid images, for there was no one total reality or placement that satisfied me—each drawing of Aaron reflected a different subjectivity, whether as a result of my differing interpretations and gestures, or my perception of his different moods.

Perhaps, alternatively, my questioning began with the works of *Claire as Naomi* (2003), in which I depicted the sitter/subject with reference to the biblical character Naomi. I did not 'dress up' my sitter as the biblical character. My interest was in approaching her as if she were someone else's story. At the same time it was inescapable that I was working with the image of Claire—there was nothing in the image to indicate that this subject was Naomi. The only indication was in the title of the work. I was experimenting with notions of identity in representation, questioning what actually constitutes identity in the image.

My explorations seemed to clearly indicate that I was not satisfied with depicting a fixed image of a person. All my depictions displayed shifts of movement in form and gesture, continuous material layering, at times to the point of erasure. The look of my subject was either uncannily familiar or particular yet anonymous.

By the time I was developing the 2008 body of work presented below, I was recognising these characteristics as purposeful elements of what I termed as *diasporic consciousness*: elements that arise from common experiences of diaspora. The materials I use in my portraits and in methods of application enact a mobile and ambivalent state of being that is a feature of diasporic consciousness. These transient states of imagery can be viewed as progressions or fragments of a whole. As in the *Aaron* portraits, my processes and material practice create layered images that are at once marked with gestures and stains, and erased by those marks and stains. Erasure is a significant metaphor for the diasporic experience of loss, with its own traces of marks and stains, where place and time are continuously recreated and relocated in memory and identification.

The subjects of these portraits are interrelated in image and through biological connection. Each image is made up of two referents. One I term the sitter, who has come to my studio to sit for the portrait. The other is drawn from a photograph of a parent or child of the sitter, taken from a time outside the parameters of this project. In self-critique, I ask how I can use the photograph as a portrayal equal in human presence to the sitter whose presence I have experienced beyond the image. In answer, I remind myself that it is not the essence of the human behind the photograph that I am portraying but rather the image of an absent person I know has a significant presence in a relationship they have with the person visiting my studio.

My use of the familial relationships of my subjects in works that incorporate photography, photocopy and drawing proposes a construction not only of a familial subjectivity but of a relational portrait that is simultaneously self and other. The portrait includes my relationship to the sitter and the image of the absent other, while giving heightened attention to the relationship *between* the two subjects. My drawing attempts to portray particularity, not so much within the facial features or expression of the person depicted as in what the relationship between sitter and imaged absent other instigates within my own artistic practice.

In *MotherDaughter (as self-portrait)* (2008) (Figure 3.4) each image is made up of my mother's photographed face as an enlarged photocopy transfer together with the observational drawing of parts of my face layered over parts of her face. The areas of watercolour wash surrounding the face have been sandpapered in some places in an attempt to excavate an underlying physical presence.

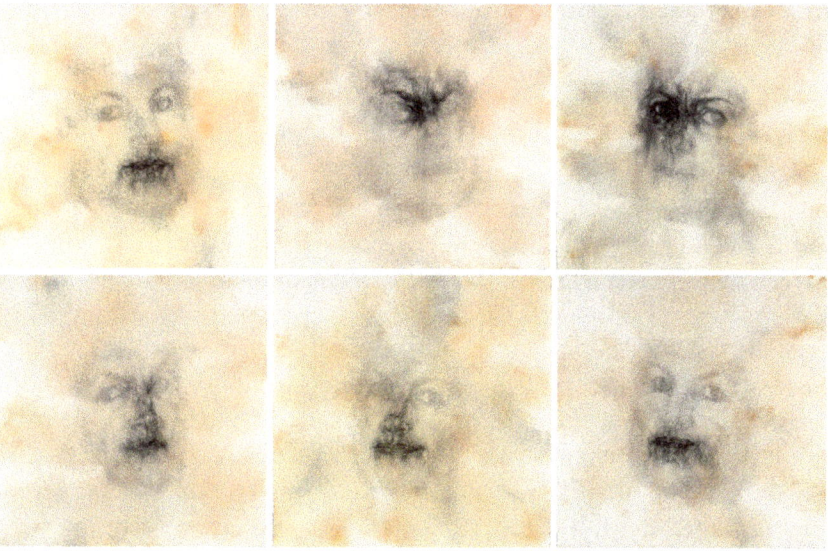

Figure 3.4: *MotherDaughter (as self-portrait)*, Gali Weiss, 2008, watercolour, solvent transfer, charcoal, graphite, 75 x 75 cm each of 6 panels.
Source: Courtesy of the artist.

At first glance, this portrait may be understood as a hybrid or composite of two people. As my portraiture work evolved I began to recognise the complexities of my subjects both as representations and in their referentiality. I had complicated the notion of the portrait's indexical quality by using a doubling of reference, whereby one reference was to the sitter present in my studio and the other to a person related to the sitter, referenced through their depiction in a photograph. The photographic image was photocopied and subsequently transferred onto paper so that reference was made not to the origin of 'person' but to the origin of 'photograph'. Additionally, new subjectivities and relationships were being constructed through the multiple images of the doubling of the subject.

My work draws two subjects into the completion of one portrait that is composed of a number of parts. These parts have in turn been assembled out of variations of repeated images of the two subjects. However, the intent of doubling in my work (the portrait of two people as one) is neither to 'return' to a single referent nor to substitute one being for another. Rather, the oscillation and shifting emphasis of the imagery calls into question the hierarchy of one subject overlaying or displacing the other; the image as well as the subject is at the same time unified and separate, lost and found, present and absent, coming in and out of focus.

Thus while my portraits can be viewed as composites or hybrids, my own experience as maker and viewer simultaneously is of the portrait as a meeting point: of two individual subjects connected by a shared history, heritage and family, and myself as artist/viewer. As both artist and viewer, mark-maker and mark-observer, I am engaging in turn with a relationship that is re-established imaginatively on paper by enacting possibilities for 'meeting' within representation. This 'meeting', in the representation of the subject's facial features, will never bring about a unified whole, but the making and identifying within the process of production—the mark-making and trace—can present the possibility of 'oneness' or completeness. Identifying with the process of production does not mean interpreting the signs of the mark-making but rather re-enacting the processes of materiality that are open to being engaged with imaginatively. In this way, the viewer is invited to enter into that process of possibilities through *identification*, rather than by *recognising* an identity.

3. DIASPORIC LOOKING

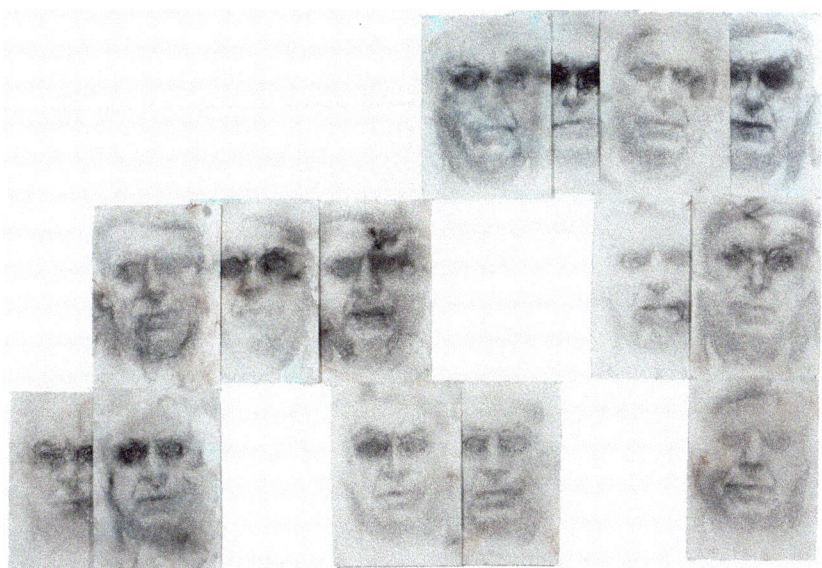

Figure 3.5: *FatherDaughter*, Gali Weiss, 2008, ink and watercolour wash, solvent transfer, charcoal, graphite, 52.5 x 37 cm each of 14 panels.
Source: Courtesy of the artist.

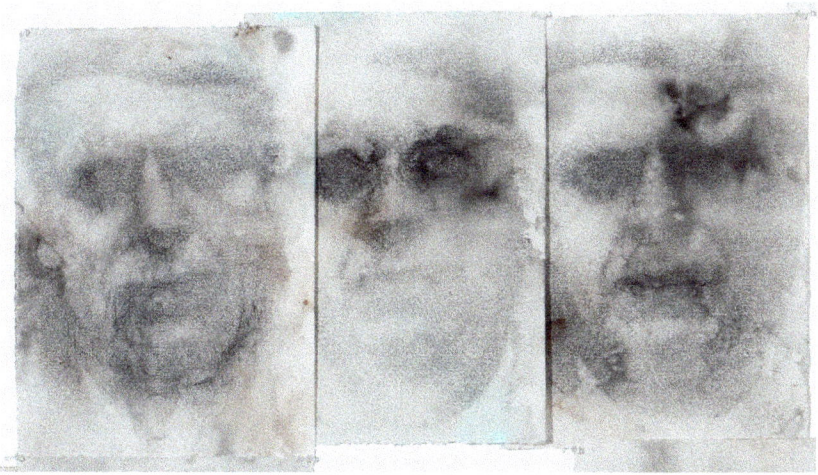

Figure 3.5a: *FatherDaughter* (detail), Gali Weiss, 2008, ink and watercolour wash, solvent transfer, charcoal, graphite, 52.5 x 37 cm each of 14 panels.
Source: Courtesy of the artist.

IMAGING IDENTITY

As with *MotherDaughter*, *FatherDaughter* (2008) and *MotherSon* (2008) (Figures 3.5 and 3.6) present a relational portrait of parent and child, only this time ambivalence extends to displacement in gender. *FatherDaughter* is a wall installation of 14 panels. The source image of the 'father', the absent subject, is a small photograph in which he poses at a distance from the photographer. The eyes of the subject are in shadow. The marks of drawing are of observational drawing in my studio of the 'daughter', at much the same age as that of the father at the moment of being photographed. While much of the focus is drawn to the eyes, my focus is not limited to the eyes but extends to the whole installation and viewing experience. My focus is multiple, for I am dealing with looking and the look returned, with the spaces between the forms of the individual faces and across as well as within the viewing trajectories of the installation as a whole.

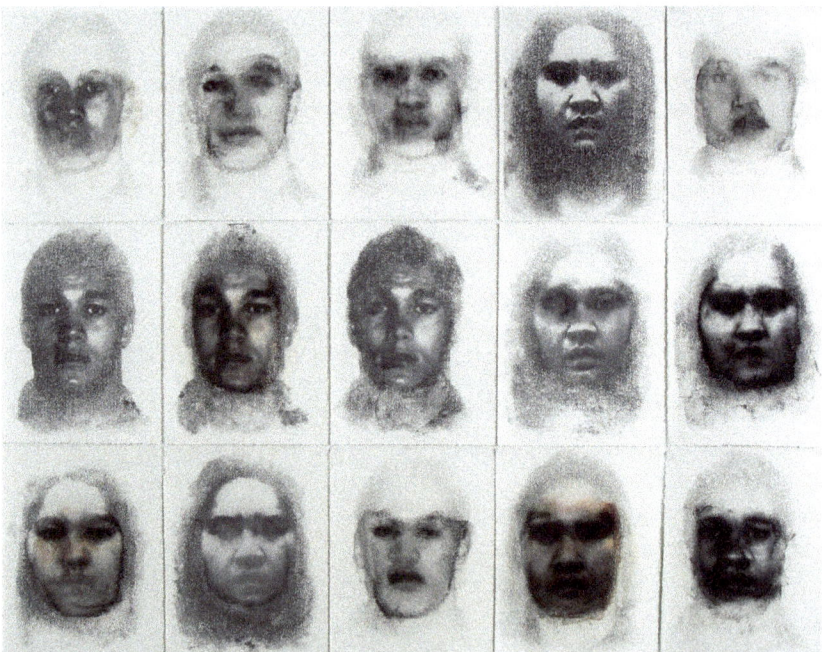

Figure 3.6: *MotherSon*, Gali Weiss, 2008, solvent transfer, graphite, 37 x 30 cm each of 15 panels.
Source: Courtesy of the artist.

The images in *MotherSon* (2008) comprise two photographs that have been photocopied and transferred to paper. The original photograph of the 'son' was a small digital print given to me by the 'mother', whom I photographed myself. As in all these portraits, an image of one subject is overlaid with an image of another in various layers, sizes and emphases. Rather than the mark-making of observational drawing, artistic choices regarding material application and chance actions were the crucial interventions in this series. Mine is not only a visual and interpretive relationship with the photograph but also a material relationship via my transferring of the photograph to paper. In undertaking this manipulation of the image and carrying it across in a newly mediated form to establish a relationship with the sitter's image, I attempt to create a space that involves another relationship to the image—that of the viewer.

Materially, the photograph presents me with the stillness of past time captured. The photocopied photograph becomes a tool for thought. It presents me with possibilities for present and future imaging and imagining. The photocopy is transferred onto paper, at times in several layers, with differing manipulations. What is left is the trace of the photograph, which had the trace of the subject, captured at a particular time in a particular place. By using the (photo)copy I am not trying to represent the absent referent, nor the photograph. My intent, rather, is to free up the referent from the context of the photograph into a new imagery in order to interact with him/her as animated presence. One could say that I am setting up a challenge: to diffuse the 'deadness'[31] of the posed subject and to diffuse the distant 'other', through my material interactions and through the relational positioning of the subject-images. Continual interaction activates this relational presence, not by interacting with the 'pose', which is the face's expression or place, but through the evocation of a dialogue with a human face as subject. The copy mediates between the 'real', stilled subject and myself as artist because the image comes alive as subject in the artistic process of production.

---

31 Here I use 'dead' in the sense that Roland Barthes gives to the subject position of the photograph, as the person poses for the camera, thereby creating him/herself as other, and thus transforming him/herself into an image: as 'a subject who feels he is becoming an object, I experience a kind of death'. 'I have become Death in person.' Roland Barthes, *Camera lucida: Reflections on photography*, trans. Richard Howard, New York, Farrar, Straus and Giroux, 1981, p. 14.

IMAGING IDENTITY

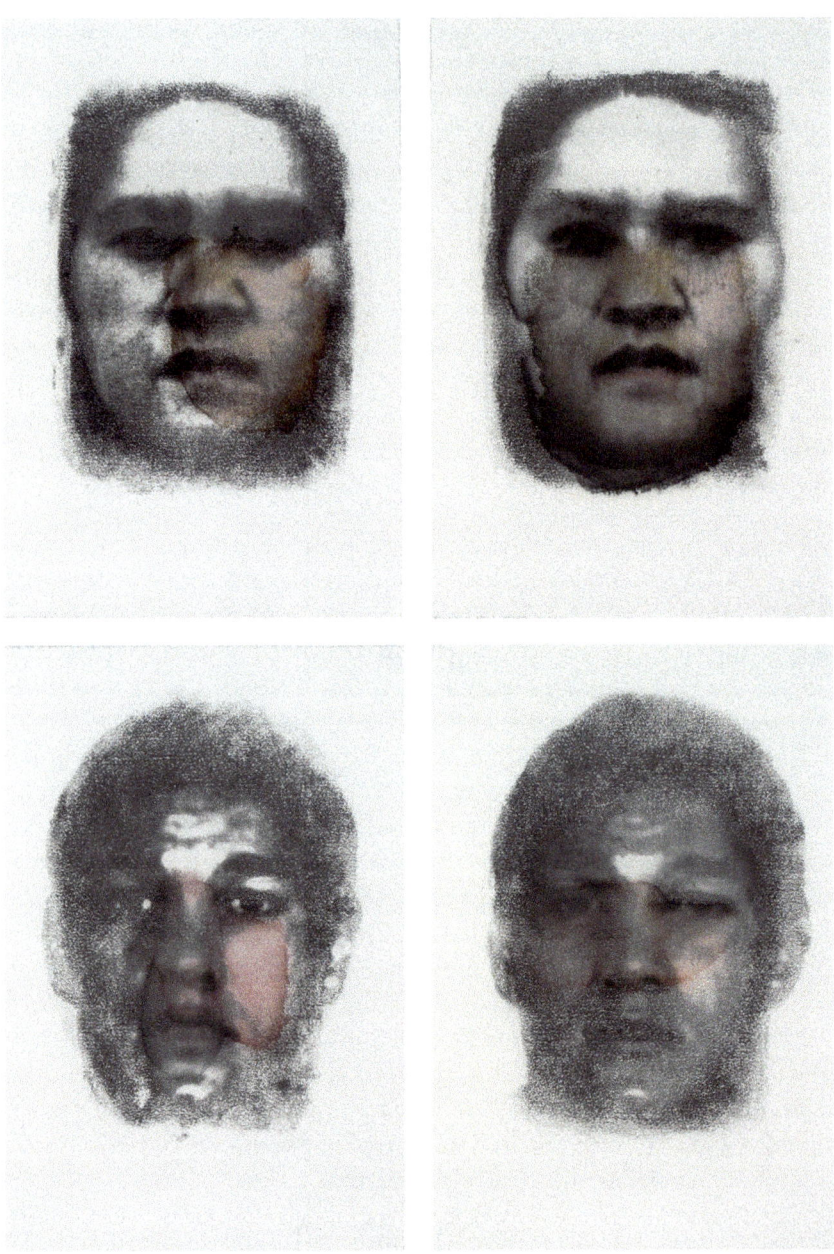

Figure 3.7: *MotherSon II*, Gali Weiss, 2008, black & white and colour solvent transfer, 60 x 40.5 cm each of four panels.
Source: Courtesy of the artist.

In *MotherSon II* (2008) (Figure 3.7), facial expression occurs not through features but through the action and placement of material elements. The border of a stain, for example, affects the expression of a feature of the face. In this way, the portrait shifts from being an iconic object that has a life-presence of its own, or that represents the uniqueness or essence of the person outside it, to function as a site of mediation and negotiation, a site of relationality. In the words of Buck-Morss, my task is 'not to get behind the image surface but to stretch it, enrich it, give it definition, give it time'.[32] These portraits thus become sites of collective presence and production—in subject, material production and viewing.

Portraiture as culture

This way of construing the subjectivity of the portrait is at odds with those concerned with the portrayal of the specificity, 'truth' or 'knowledge' of the person portrayed. My primary intention is not to replace such notions of referentiality and 'authenticity' as inform the conventions of portraiture, even though my approach may challenge them. Rather, I have strived to investigate further the productive possibilities of portraiture, 'rethinking' the portrait alongside other current 'rethinkings' of culture, identity and representation.

Avtar Brah suggests that cultures are processes rather than 'reified artefacts'.[33] Her argument suggests a parallel viewing of portraiture as itself a culture, where the genre can be seen to have a history, a genealogy, an authority and conventions of language and practice. Thus representations that do not comply with the historical, essentialist criteria of portraiture—portraits that, for example, are anonymous yet nevertheless images of persons—need not be viewed as marginal or challenging to the genre, but rather help constitute the genre itself.

The site of portraiture can accommodate works that subscribe to the ideals of unity, homogeneity and pure presence, as well as those that declare the subjective impossibility of such qualities. In this way the space of portraiture can parallel the space of diaspora, or culture at large, where works (and people) that enact a desire for

---
32 Buck-Morss, 1991, p. 25.
33 Brah, 1996, p. 92.

unity can co-exist with works (and people) that refute the possibility of fixed and unified positions, but stop short of rejecting tradition.[34] Hence, portraiture can be understood not so much as a genre within the boundaries of a territory that includes or excludes but rather as a cultural site that contextualises the desire for, in Brah's words, a 'politics of identification'.[35]

By conjoining portraiture and diaspora, I 'think through' notions of identity, subjectivity and representation. My work plays with layered possibilities of subjectivity—with notions of multiplicity, erasure, location and dislocation, of mobility and ambivalence, of self and other, working from a premise of inheritance. Beyond the qualities of transience in the portraits is the figuring of a space in which past and present meet in new formations. The sense of inheritance, of the past that is integral to diasporic consciousness and that includes imaginings of home in place and time, and of futurity, is highlighted in my work through the doubling of subjects and creation of a space of relationality between them.

The completed portraits suggest imprints of memory and postmemory through the duality of subjects but also through the selection of materials and media. The selection and application of materials and processes of production are integral to both the thinking and becoming of diasporic personhood: the photocopy as the copy of a photograph, itself a reproduction, a trace of body, time and place; the adaptive transferring by hand of the photocopy, which at times results in a reductive linear mark, at others a stain alluding to corporeal qualities; the charcoal and graphite gestures of observational drawing that trace the artist's visual trajectory as marks of repetitive exploration, discovery, formation; the paper itself, which lacks demarcation when used as overlapping panels (Figure 3.5) or as a layer and disintegration of a layer between images (Figure 3.8).[36] The materials are employed not simply as a means of constructing a representation but also as an enactment of that representation, in all its relational aspects.

---

34 Andrew Benjamin, *Art, mimesis and the avant-garde*, London and New York, Routledge, 1991, pp. 63–4.
35 Brah, 1996, p. 93.
36 One feature of *MotherSon III* is the result of the photocopy solvent transfer being applied to the other side of the paper, absorbing into the paper and revealing itself on the viewed side.

3. DIASPORIC LOOKING

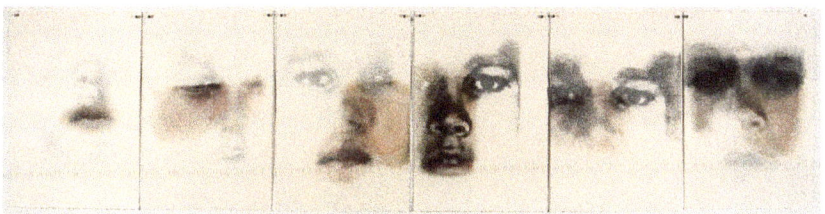

Figure 3.8: *MotherSon III*, Gali Weiss, 2008, black & white and colour solvent transfer, 60 x 40.5 cm each panel.
Source: Courtesy of the artist.

My works attempt to create imaginative possibilities for a dynamic portrayal in a 'still' representation through a relational approach to the portrait as representation and as presence. These portrayals offer simultaneously a collective and an individual representation of personhood and a viewing experience that is participatory—based on identification rather than identity. They contain qualities and address themes that are prevalent within diasporic consciousness and that are commonly experienced as paradoxes of diasporic life: the simultaneity of difference and sameness, location and dislocation, belonging and otherness, particularity and anonymity. Like diasporic space, which encompasses those who leave as well as those who stay and those who return, portraiture can provide a potent space for enacting multiple and transient experiences of presence through which to negotiate the 'home' of authenticity.

PART II: Interfaces

4

The self-portrait and the film and video essay

John Conomos

> The world is but a perennial movement. All things in it are in constant motion … I cannot keep my subject still … I do not portray being, I portray passing … [1]

Born under a Claude Neon milk-bar sign

This essay seeks to illuminate the intertwined forms of the essay and the self-portrait and does so in light of recent currents in contemporary art, film, and literary and media theory. Today we can speak not only of the essay film but also of the video essay and, more generally, of the essayistic in postmodern digital creativity. As a media artist, I have always been attracted to the essay form because of its pliable, intertextual capacity to act, as Serge Daney would have it, as a 'go-between', linking cinema, video, new media, literature and critical theory.[2] I have been fascinated with the idea of

---

1 Michel de Montaigne, 'Of repentance', in *The complete essays*, trans. MA Screech, London, Penguin, 1993.
2 For a more elaborate discussion of Serge Daney's idea of a filmmaker, artist and writer as a 'go-between', and the broader implications for contemporary art, cinema and literature, see John Conomos, *Mutant media*, Sydney, Artspace/Power Publications, 2008. And for the actual concept of 'go-between' as defined by Daney see his *Postcards from the cinema*, trans. Paul Grant, London and New York, Berg, 2007.

cinema, video and installation as writing. The phantasmatic notion of film and video as a form of sound–image–performance–writing has haunted me since the 1960s (think of the work of Chantal Akerman, Jean Cocteau, Jean-Luc Godard, Chris Marker, Agnes Varda, Yvonne Rainer and Orson Welles).[3] Over many years I have made videos, films, installations and radio as a diasporic Greek-Australian subject in postwar Australia. I have sought to create audio-visual self-portraits in the French New Wave tradition of Alexandre Astruc's key concept of *caméra-stylo* cinema.[4]

Autobiography, landscape, memory, time and the self-portrait have been interrelated concerns of my art and writing practice since the 1970s. And over the years the self-portrait has been particularly central to my videotapes, media installations, radiophonic essays and photo-performance. This (post)modern genre par excellence of image-making is emblematic of the underlying conceptual, formal and technological ideas, contexts and forms that have emerged since the historical avant-garde. As artist and writer, I have been substantially engaged with creating 'in-between' contexts, ideas and genres that emanate from art, cinema, literature, philosophy and critical theory. Indeed, it is because I have been excavating precisely these very art forms, figures and contexts that I have been able to engage in an autobiographical/critical project over the last four decades.

But it is not that simple, for I am also critically interested in questions of seeing and hearing that may hover beyond our present horizons of creative, cultural and existential possibility. The essay form has allowed me to fashion videos, films, installations and radio texts in the hope of sustaining an informed, speculative and poetic 'border-crossing' between established art forms and more recent forms that are particularly salient to contemporary art. In other words, I have pursued the production of trans-media work that critiques the binary essentialism of (post)modernism and western thought. At the outset, it should be observed that the increasingly compelling terrain of essayistic cinema (including the diary film, the notebook film and

---

3   For a discussion of the general concept of cinema, video and new media as a kind of image–sound–performance–writing as it may apply to the works of Jean-Luc Godard, Orson Welles, Chris Marker, Jean Cocteau and Agnes Varda, see Conomos, 2008.

4   For a clear and concise introduction to Alexandre Astruc's *caméra-stylo* idea of a personal form of cinema in the context of the French New Wave cinema, see Richard Neupert, *A history of the French New Wave cinema*, 2nd edn, Madison, The University of Wisconsin Press, 2002, pp. 45–56.

the essay film in general), video and new media is critically indebted to Michel Montaigne's concept of the literary essay, as well as to autobiography and the self-portrait in painting. Image-making in this evolving field of creativity is personal—intimate cinema/video/new media trembling with experimental risk-taking and crossing generic boundaries without need of a passport.[5]

I became interested in creating art that questions itself as a continuing autobiographical project and articulates an overall attempt to be self-reflexive and open-ended, a project always striving to remind us that art is power and needs always to be 'untimely', to put it in Nietzsche's terms.[6] Art, for me, is anti-art. The essay form permits the artist-writer to be a self-interrogator, and the past to be recognised, crucially, as a part of the present. And yet art and writing for me share a perennially nagging, half-glimpsed striving towards an undecided elsewhere.[7]

It is in this critical context that the essay form in contemporary audio-visual production has given me hope. In the 1970s, while squatting in London, I encountered a 'popular front' ethos—*à la* Jean Renoir's *Crime of Monsieur Lange*—of 'in-between' creativity and living. And video was always at the centre of this. In that era of punk, people used video as art, social critique, performance and parody. Returning to Sydney in 1977, I attended several short courses on video editing and production techniques. The liquid collage and intertextual poetry of the electronic medium bewitched me. It was so calligraphically flexible—just like seeing sign-writers applying their ornate art to my parents' milk-bar window in the 1950s, advertising our coming weekly bargains. To me this was to make images as if putting pen to paper, celluloid, video and neon. Enchantment.

Our milk bar at Tempe became a Bachelardian theatre of bicultural being, dislocation, surreal reverie, silence, memory and otherness. It indelibly coloured my understanding of a poetics of 'in-between' creativity, foreignness and discordances of time and space. The milk bar as home, as an uncanny place of estrangement and wonderment,

---

5   This notion of 'travelling without a passport' is drawn from the work of Steve Fagin. See Peter Wollen, 'An interview with Steve Fagin', *October*, no. 41, Summer, 1987, p. 99.
6   Friedrich Wilhelm Nietzsche, *Untimely Meditations*, Cambridge, Cambridge University Press, 1997.
7   In this I am inspired by the work of Maurice Blanchot, Hugh Kenner and Ezra Pound.

defined my life, as in Michel de Certeau's words, 'being in between'.[8] I was always aware of being a hybrid alien. In grappling with and indeed surviving the cultural and ideological contradictions and fictions of my life, Stanley Cavell's idea of 'the strangeness of oneself' has resonated strongly.[9] Through cunning, language, mimicry and play, I learnt to value cinephilia, difference, exilic marginality, self-reflexivity and experimentation in order to survive—to make sense of my ongoing life as a hyphenated being: Greek-Australian, artist-writer. I would cling to essays, fragments, aphorisms, quotes, digressions, autobiographies and mémoires like a marooned sailor does floating wreckage. All of my works, whether *Autumn song*, *Album leaves*, *Shipwreck* or *The spiral of time*, in their respective aesthetic, cultural and formal ways enact my interest in subjective cinema—the self-portrait and the essay film and video form.

As a reluctant, introspective child acting as a scribe for our many ethnic customers in their Kafkaesque dealings with bureaucracies—the local council, the law, education, immigration and so on—I intuitively realised that life as an immigrant, as the other, meant absurdity, solitude and vulnerability (hence also my deep interest in American film noir). Waiting for the next customer to enter through the door of the milk bar—always waiting—I would watch that doorway magically transform into a movie screen, framing a world of enchantment beyond. Busy images of passing cars, customers, shopping, screaming kids and teenagers doing their Jukebox Cindy Sherman thing—I would dearly caress every image framed by the door with my roving, fugitive eyes.

Ever since those days, I have been engaged in the risk-taking enterprise of creating 'in-between' media art and writing anchored in Rainer Maria Rilke's belief that the artist or writer is the bearer of cultural memory.[10] Making memory matter: this is paramount in my praxis as an artist-scholar-writer. I create art as works against forgetting. But as we are all too aware, as individuals we often misremember art, cinema, literature and life. How much do we misremember? This question haunts all of us and is lyrically posed by one of England's

---

8   Michel de Certeau, *The practice of everyday life*, trans. Steven Rendell, Berkeley, University of California Press, 2007.
9   Stanley Cavell, *A pitch of philosophy*, Cambridge, MA, Harvard University Press, 1994, p. xv.
10   Raymond Bellour, *Between-the-images*, trans. Allyn Hardyck, Zurich, JRP/Ringier, 2011.

great film and video essayists, Chris Petit, in his 1999 'road-movie' video essay *Negative space*, a homage to late, great film critic and painter Manny Farber.

Writing and making art for me is utterly compelling, ontological. I have no choice; I do not know what else to do. Kafka once described his nocturnal feverish writing as an act of 'interior emigration'. Caught between two worlds I would always read between languages, between cultures, between art forms. I have been doing this all my life; rummaging among the dustbins of various art forms, genres and cultural contexts. By existential necessity I am—in the classic European sense of the term—a 'ragpicker'.[11] Or if you will, I became an 'aesthetic vagabond',[12] interested in the multiplying 'creative encounters'[13] that have been or are taking place between art, cinema, video and the new media technologies. I am concerned with the conversations that exist between these different art forms, contexts and genres, locating, as it were, the ancients next to the moderns in the same room and seeing what might ensue (think of Octavio Paz or Michel Serres).[14] For me, analogue and digital media coexist as part of a continuous dialogue of art-making.

The essay film and video essay

Writing of the audio-visual essay in film, video art and new media arts, we can trace its historical legacy to the literary, the philosophical and the photographic—from Michel Montaigne through Theodor Adorno and Walter Benjamin to James Agee and Walker Evans'

---

11   Walter Benjamin, *The arcades project*, trans. Howard Eiland and Kevin McLaughlin, Cambridge, Harvard University Press, 2002; Georg Simmel, 'The metropolis and mental life', in *The sociology of Georg Simmel*, New York, Free Press, 1976.
12   Jean-Louis Schefer, *The enigmatic body*, Cambridge, Cambridge University Press, 2000, p. 4.
13   Gilles Deleuze and Félix Guattari, *A thousand plateaus: Capitalism and schizophrenia*, trans. Brian Massumi, London, Athlone, 1987.
14   Here I am influenced especially by Octavio Paz and Michel Serres. See, for example, Octavio Paz, *On poets and others*, New York, Seaver Books, 1986; Michel Serres, *The troubadour of knowledge*, Ann Arbour, University of Michigan Press, 1997.

classic collaboration *Let us now praise famous men*.[15] For Montaigne, the essay was an ideal vehicle for speculating aloud and testing ideas on paramount questions of life, culture, politics, human fragility and society. It also asked questions of his own subjectivity and, by focusing on the dialectical tensions between 'fact' and 'fiction', was able to contribute significantly to a highly elastic personal genre of creative thought and speculation.[16] The genre has the ability to compress together, in a non-systematic fashion, such devices as collage, irony, pastiche, satire, humour and paradox.

It was, however, the German critics and philosophers of the early twentieth century who further articulated what an essay might be.[17] Although it was the Hungarian Marxist Georg Lukacs who described the written essay as 'criticism as a form of art' and as a 'philosophical poem', and who thought of it as a flexible form of the 'accidental' and the 'necessary',[18] it was Adorno who took up Lukacs' ideas and characterised the genre as having the key characteristics of 'luck', 'play' and 'irrationality'. Thus for Lukacs and Adorno the essay did not put forward truth claims, as did documentary film, but was characterised by its fragmentary, wandering concerns and stylistics.

The film essay was first introduced as a concept by the German experimental filmmaker Hans Richter in April 1940.[19] Richter argued in his seminal text, 'The essay film: A new form of documentary film', that this new genre would allow the filmmaker to make the 'invisible' world of ideas and thoughts visible on the screen.[20] The film essay would transgress the traditional concepts and forms of documentary cinema, enabling the artist/filmmaker to be irrational, contradictory, speculative and fantastic—in short, to question the binary logic of western representation in art, culture, language and society.

---

15 The literature on the essay film and video has started to expand in the last few years. Previously it was lean pickings for anyone interested in the subject. The following are recommended: Noral Alter, 'Translating the essay into film and installation', *Visual Culture*, vol. 6, no. 1, 2007, pp. 44–57; Raymond Bellour, *Eye for I: Video self-portraits*, New York, Independent Curators Inc., 1989; Conomos, 2008; Timothy Corrigan, *The essay film*, Oxford and New York, Oxford University Press, 2011; and Laura Rascaroli, *The personal camera*, London and New York, Wallflower Press, 2009.
16 See Alter, 2007, pp. 49–50 and Corrigan, 2011.
17 Corrigan, 2011, pp. 21–3.
18 Georg Luckacs, *Soul And Form*, trans. Anna Bostock, Massachusetts, Cambridge University Press, 1974.
19 Corrigan, 2011, p. 63.
20 Corrigan, 2011, p. 61.

4. THE SELF-PORTRAIT AND THE FILM AND VIDEO ESSAY

In the late 1940s, there were several significant turning points in the unfolding sociocultural and aesthetic formations and contexts that substantially helped to usher in the film essay, and around two decades later, the video essay. In his famous 1948 essay 'The birth of the new avant-garde: The *caméra-stylo*', critic, filmmaker and novelist Alexandre Astruc argued that it was quite possible for a filmmaker or an artist 'to express his thoughts, however abstract they may be, or translate his obsessions exactly as he does in the contemporary essay or novel'.[21] For Astruc, the filmmaker's camera could become the equivalent of the author's pen, introducing the influential concept of the *caméra-stylo*, which animated the auteur theory of the French New Wave—exemplified by Jean-Luc Godard—and its authorial assumptions about cinematic subjectivity.

There has been no filmmaker more intertwined with the fate of the image than Godard; no one so compelled to create a new poetics of image-making anchored in the dialectic between literature and writing and the cinema (and, more recently, video). From the beginning, Godard's involvement with cinema was with its other, which for him, from the late 1950s and early 1960s on, was television. For Godard, television represented new ways of seeing and hearing, new modalities of composition and decomposition (accelerating and slowing down the image), new strategies of mise-en-scène. In a word, television's other—'video' or 'the electronic image'—for him signified an unexplored potential for locating new sites in the image.

Since *Ici et ailleurs* (1974), Godard has expanded his experimentation with the new electronic image and sound systems in order to 'redefine representation in reference to bodies, time, space and speech'.[22] Godard's 'border-crossing' activity over the last three decades has taken us into a new territory of imaginative possibilities between film and video predicated on attempting to see 'not this or that, but only to see if there is something to see'.[23] The 'writerly attributes' of the highly elastic video medium are ideal for Godard, and for other artists, including Robert Cahen, Thierry Kuntzel, Chris Marker, Steve

---

21 Corrigan, 2011, p. 65.
22 Philippe Dubois, 'Video thinks what cinema creates', in Raymond Bellour and Mary Lea Bandy (eds), *Jean-Luc Godard son + image 1974–1991*, New York, Museum of Modern Art, 1992, pp. 169–85.
23 Conomos, 'Border crossings: Jean-Luc Godard as video essayist', in *Mutant media*, 2008, pp. 133–45.

Fagin and Irit Batsry, who seek to construct a poetic style of electronic image-making, influenced by Stéphane Mallarmé, among others. These artists share a sustained interest in exploring the idea of *video-stylo* writing (following Astruc's *caméra-stylo* in cinema) in today's media arts.

Chris Marker, like Godard, uses video technology as a 'camera-pen' to create and think, and to interrogate the image (often archival) of history, politics, time and memory. Marker's enigmatic work—films, travel books, imaginary film scripts, photo-novels, videos, installations, photographs and travel essays—constitutes a highly subjective voyage across the world and its labyrinthine features of faces, landscapes, objects and animals in memory, time and space. He wanders the world recording his impressions as a furtive lyrical flâneur, reporting meditative image–sound letters that chronicle life as a vertigo of space and time linked by the insane impossibility and unreliability of memory. Marker's early film essays, such as *Dimanche à Pékin* (1955) and *Lettre de Siberie* (1957), his science-fiction short *La jetée* (1962), as well as his more personal, epistolary works such as *Sans soleil* (1983), *AK* (1985) and *Le tombeau d'Alexandre* (1992), are some of the more elaborate and haunting examples of *film-* and *video-stylo* creativity as 'autobiographical documentary' in contemporary audio-visual media.[24]

In the context of the rise of the essay film or film essay, the works of the artists I have briefly surveyed here are salient, as is the expanding significance of the essay form (both print and audio-visual) that is rapidly becoming a crucial aspect of DVDs and their supplements.[25] The legacy of the essay form is highly visible and arguably it is playing an essential role in shaping today's DVD cinephilia and its attendant global media culture. As a genre, the film and video essay problematises the cultural politics of representation and knowledge production. The essayistic in our 'post-human' moving image

---

24 Marker's essayistic work includes influential new media contributions such as the CD-ROM *Immemory*, 1997. See Catherine Lupton, *Chris Marker: Memories of the future*, London, Reaktion Books, 2008, p. 205; Conomos, 'The spiral of time: Chris Marker and new media', in *Mutant media*, 2008, pp. 183–95.

25 It is interesting to note the development of the scholarly video essay phenomenon of the last two years or so. No doubt the reasons for this new pedagogic essay form are complicated, but one may be able to trace a vital link to its origins in terms of the supplements (documentaries on filmmakers and written essays, etc.) of a given DVD. This new essay form in film and media scholarship warrants further critical scrutiny.

culture is self-reflexive in that, by its very inter-disciplinary nature, it offers its own film and video criticism. Like its distant cousin the philosophical literary essay, the film and video essay embodies cross-disciplinary concepts, forms and norms. Essentially, it does not adhere to a linear narrative trajectory, but rather is hybrid, open-ended and non-hierarchical in its pluralistic image–sound–spatial figurations. This spiralling, hesitant and introspective form of image-making connects to what Chris Marker once described as 'the imaginary country which spreads out inside us'.[26]

As someone who has been working in the essay form and the self-portrait (across literature, cinema and video), crossing so many different kinds of cultural, generic, linguistic and psychic borders in my life's journey has been dear to me. As Salman Rushdie once said, 'To see things plainly, you have to cross a frontier'.[27] Easier said than done. I have always regarded art-making (irrespective of the medium) a fugitive, elliptical enterprise that questions one's own aesthetic, cultural and epistemological baggage. The artist-writer as self-interrogator, as trickster, crosses the thresholds of multiple forms, always attempting to dig deep, to mingle things, perennially engaged in boundary-creation and boundary-crossing.[28]

Thus it is wise to note that the critique of amnesia as a mass-mediated malady of late-capitalist culture is not new in itself, as Andreas Huyssen points out. For example, witness Adorno's, Walter Benjamin's and Martin Heidegger's interwar writings on the obsession with memory and the fetish quality of mass cultural forms.[29] Yet, my work as an artist and as a critic/theorist strives to underscore how today's cybernetic virus of amnesia is threatening to consume memory. This contemporary amnesia constantly blights our cultural and epistemological endeavours to speak of video art's mutating complexities in a digital age. Lamentably, this amnesia is systematically embedded in our academic, funding and museological institutions and their theoretical frameworks of interpretation. Cultural amnesia travels by way of computer-networked media in our age of hyper-consumption, information networks and global capital.

---

26 Marker, cited in Conomos, 2008, p. 191.
27 Salman Rushdie, *Imaginary homelands*, London, Granta Books, 1991, p. 125.
28 Lewis Hyde, *Trickster makes the world*, Edingburgh, Canongate, 2008, p. 7.
29 Andreas Huyssen, *Twilight memories: Marking time in a culture of amnesia*, New York, Routledge, 1995.

When speaking of video art and new media, it is vital to deal with their complexities, temporalities and cultural logics. For as Hubert Damisch reminded Denis Hollier, Yves-Alain Bois and Rosalind Krauss, ' We live in a moment of suspension. Is it the end of something or the beginning of something else?'[30] Damisch's remarks have been profoundly salient to my critical understanding of our emergent moving-image culture. In relation to the paradoxical art form we call video, for instance, we still lack the hermeneutic ability to speak of it in a language that is as inventive as it is practised today in its mutable forms of representation-production, exhibition and critical reception. I agree with Sean Cubitt, Chris Darke, Siegfried Zielinski and Nicholas Zurbrugg, among others, that we simply do not know how to talk about video art's histories, contexts, genres and effects.

Nicholas Zurbrugg's concluding words to his incisive 1991 critique of Fredric Jameson's distorted exegesis of postmodern video and multimedia performance—that we (all of us) need to learn how to observe, analyse, interpret and evaluate the new arts of the 1980s and 1990s, and now in these first decades of the new century— lamentably have still not been heeded.[31] For me, video art is not dead. Along with Zielinski and others, I maintain that we are ignorant of the art form—aesthetically, archivally, curatorially and pedagogically—particularly of our own video creations since the 1970s, as they are tragically (and tiresomely) eclipsed by the Euro-American canon of the art form.

To speak of one's own art and writing practice in the context of Australian video art and new media is quite a tricky thing to do, given what Gilles Deleuze demonstrated when he persuasively spelled out the many intricate biographical, cultural, social and philosophical complexities central to the act of explaining one's self to any given audience.[32] This was perfectly illustrated for me when one day in the early 1980s I watched on my television set Jean Genet being interviewed by a BBC television crew. Within minutes Genet, in his withering scatalogical way, upturned the proverbial applecart

---

30 See Yves-Alain Bois, Denis Hollier and Rosalind Krauss, 'A conversation with Hubert Damisch', *October*, Summer, 1998, p. 16.
31 Nicholas Zurbrugg, 'Jameson's complaint: Video art and the inter-textual "time-wall"', *Screen*, vol. 32, no. 1, Spring, 1991, pp. 16–34.
32 Gilles Deleuze and Claire Parnet, *Dialogues*, trans. Hugh Tomlinson and Barbara Hammerjam, New York, Columbia University Press, 1987.

and interrogated the interviewer about the ideological fictions and limitations of what conducting an interview signifies. What was it to explain oneself to someone else via the customary 'ingrained' generic banalities of television?

I became, in Abul R JanMohamed's sense, a 'border' video-maker and theorist/writer, someone who has (regardless of their class, gender, political or historical determinations) occupied over the years a heterotopic, specular site in society.[33] I found myself located in a nomadic, paradoxical space between culture and system, thereby representing a subject-as-space in the hope of delineating, critiquing and inverting the real sites of the dominant culture, someone who believes in the Nietzschean self-enabling intertextual freedoms and perspectives of 'in-between' media creativity, opening up a kind of 'creative stuttering' within language.[34] I have treated image-making and writing as forms of 'travelling without a passport', as Steve Fagin would say, or as the French put it, as 'paperless'—homeless, 'without (identity) papers'. I regard both creative activities as critical-speculative enterprises, located at the edge, always in the midst of things, suspicious of monocultural homogeneity.[35]

1968 and 1984

In 1968, as a student at the University of New South Wales, I experienced two events that would shape the kind of artist, writer and educator engaged in media arts that I was to become. Thanks to Michael Glasheen (whose pioneering importance to Australian video art is yet to be given adequate critical and museological due), I walked into the Science Theatre—where I would take a subject in the history and philosophy of science (gratefully, I may add, in hindsight) because of the university's critical legacy to CP Snow's two-culture debate of the 1960s—and heard Buckminster Fuller speak.[36]

---

33 Abdul R JanMohamed, 'Wordliness-without-world, homelessness-as home: Toward a definition of the specular border intellectual', in Michael Sprinker (ed.), *Edward Said: A critical reader*, Oxford, Blackwell, 1992, p. 103.
34 Deleuze and Parnet, 1987.
35 See Wollen, 1987, p. 99.
36 CP Snow, *The Two Cultures*, London, Cambridge University Press, 1959.

There he was, like Robert Crumb's Mr Natural—snowy-haired, wearing thick black glasses and a threadbare black suit, with a clutch of biros and pencils in his front jacket pocket. He spoke for close to three hours non-stop, in his swirling, vertiginous, collage-style of verbal delivery, a labyrinthine vortex of cross-disciplinary subjects: Black Mountain College poetics, architecture, modernism, atonal music, American transcendental philosophy, Zen Buddhism, John Cage, mathematics ... I was cauterised into my seat. 'What in the name of Jesus H Christ was that?', I asked myself as I left the auditorium. Today I still think about it; its reverberations are still with me.

I had a similar experience in 1984—having by this time developed some critical, self-reflexive hermeneutic tools to deal with the encounter—when I attended Gayatri Spivak's restless, panther-like talk at the University of Sydney's Footlight Theatre during the momentous Future Fall Conference on postmodernism. Another encounter that influenced my turn to collage aesthetics had occurred, again in the Science Theatre, in 1968, when I heard French novelist and critic Michel Butor speak on Charles Baudelaire as a collagist-flâneur. Michel Butor's address, like Fuller's talk, but a much quieter, modulated style of verbal presentation, opened up exciting new vistas of creative and theoretical possibility.

In more recent times, I have come to believe that one is obliged to treat the past, the present and the future as a continuing dialogue of possibilities; that we must be alive to our one shared, turning world, treating the past as integral with the present. In other words, I put the ancients next to the moderns, producing in Paz's fitting expression, 'an antiquity without dates', and see what intertextual conversations ensue.[37] I simply do not believe in use-by-date orthodoxies relating to creativity and scholarship. 'Give me a pencil, a box of matches and some paper and I will create cinema for you', Godard once said.

---

37   Paz, 1986, p. 57.

Consequently, I have learned to value the intertextual potential that comes from an engagement of old and new media on the same shared plane of multimedia creativity. I appreciate Serres' important characterisation of the legacy of Cartesian rationalism as a violent, totalising force in our approach to the question of the relationship between Snow's two cultures and the fate of analogue media in a post-computer epoch.[38] For Serres there are complex passages that we can traverse from one domain to another, like the difficult (but rewarding) routes that he himself as a sailor-philosopher would take between isolated islands of order in a sea of chaos—as in the Northwest Passage—from one medium to another. We must be prepared to problematise global paradigms and universal ahistorical modes of thinking; to shift our ways of knowing by negotiating complexity, disorder, uncertainty and multiplicity in everyday life.

Autumn song and beyond

Finally, in concluding this essay, I wish to say a few words about my own autobiographical videographic practice and its grounding in the aesthetic and critical historical avant-garde, contemporary art, literature and philosophy. I shall focus primarily on *Autumn song*, as it is emblematic of my approach to video art, and briefly refer to my more recent work, *The spiral of time* (2013).[39]

---

38   Michel Serres, 'Northwest Passage', in Timothy Simone, Peter Caravetta, Frank Mecklenbeerg, Brigitte Ouvry-Vial, Gregory Whitehead (eds), *Oasis*, New York, Semiotext(e), 1984, p. 104.
39   On *Autumn song* see John Conomos, *Autumn song, the Kythera narratives*, Sydney, Australian Regional Media, 1999. On *The spiral of time* and other works see Brad Buckley and John Conomos, *Brad Buckley/John Conomos*, Sydney, The Australian Centre for Photography, illustrated monograph, 2013.

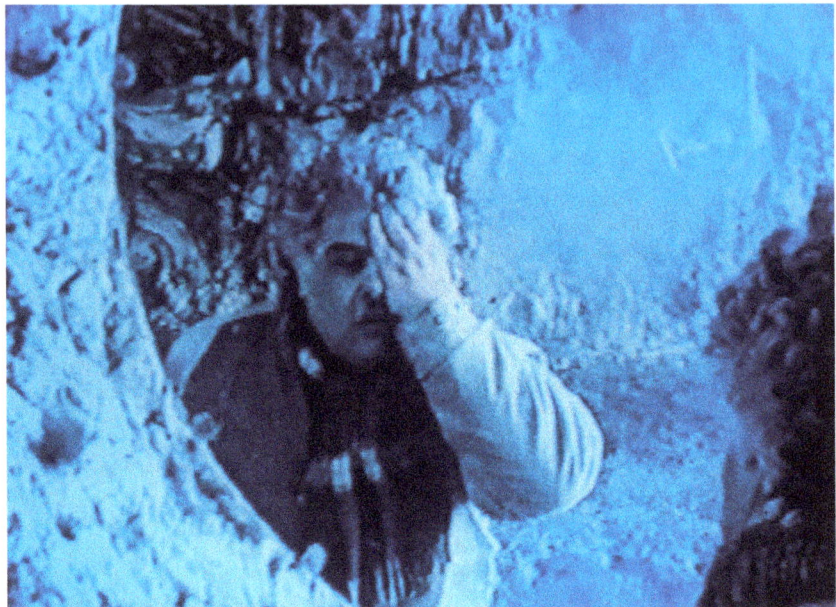

Figure 4.1: *Autumn song* (still), John Conomos, 1998, SP Beta, 23 mins duration.
Source: Courtesy of the artist.

The underlying narrative premise of *Autumn song*, as a multilayered, pun-encrusted, self-portrait video, centres on the powerful influence an uncle, Uncle Manoli, had on me as a child. He, unlike his siblings who migrated to Australia, never left the Greek island Kythera. My parents and relatives would often jokingly warn me about him—that if I wasn't careful, I'd turn out like him: a legendary, lazy, misanthropic writer with an encyclopaedic mind who spent his life in taverns playing cards. Although I didn't meet him until the 1970s (he looked like a carbon copy of my biological father, who passed away in 1957), as a child the spectre of Uncle Manoli profoundly shaped my imagination.

Autumn song's landscapes, and numerous images and quotes drawn from Man Ray, Maya Deren, Georges Franju, Buster Keaton and Chris Marker, together with its open-air performances, suggest the situation of the postcolonial alien caught between places in postwar Australia. As an autobiographical work, *Autumn song* engages various elaborate ideas of postcolonial dislocation, cultural mistranslation and transmigratory spaces. Its overall *caméro-stylo* aesthetics is predicated on video collage as defined in the context of cinematic and visual modernity and new media. Simply put, *Autumn song*, as a baroque, essayistic self-portrait, questions the surreal logic of my own (childhood) life in that it strives to problematise the conflicts, tensions and transgressive silences of my poly-cultural experience, at the same time endeavouring to define new expressive possibilities in the video medium.

One of the dominant formalistic tropes of my video weaves together references (especially in its use of film inter-titles, quotes and certain props in my improvisatory performances) to past artists, authors, filmmakers, video-makers and thinkers as a kind of antidote to the institutionalised amnesia that seems to be impacting on contemporary media's history. The voiceover (narrated by Lex Marinos) accompanying the film's improvised, playful, self-reflexive images of my childhood memories at Tempe; the numerous in situ images of me performing in the tranquil wintry landscape of Kythera (an island immortalised by Theo Angelopoulos, Baudelaire, Ernest Bloch and Claude Debussy, together with its smaller adjacent island of Anti-Kythera, which the Surrealists included in their world map); and images of me as Uncle Manoli approaches the camera with a rock, are images of the foreigner, the exiled, caught in claustrophobic spaces.

My more recent video, *The spiral of time* (2013), similarly focuses on my postcolonial subjectivity shaped by exile, longing and restlessness. But this work also amplifies how an existence that does not feel at home in society resonates deeply in the way one dwells within one's own body. In contrast to *Autumn song*'s elaborate themes, sequences and meta-generic concerns, this new video is much more compressed in its allusive, speculative, collage style and concerns. It pays tribute to art, experimental/avant-garde and classical narrative cinema, contemporary and modernist literature, cultural theory and philosophy. More specifically, *The spiral of time* pays homage to the 'trance film' of the past, and its stark black-and-white photography evokes a netherworld of existential sleepwalking and lyrical poetry.[40]

---

40 The trance film, as a genre of European art cinema and the American avant-garde/experimental cinema, has an elaborate aesthetic, cultural and historical genesis. Stan Brakhage, Jean Cocteau and Maya Deren are three of its key exemplars. Kenneth Anger's highly influential 'mytho-poetic' cinema is also relevant.

Characteristically, quotations abound, drawn from the various disciplines that have shaped the basic template of my aesthetic, creative and theoretical imagination and concerns.

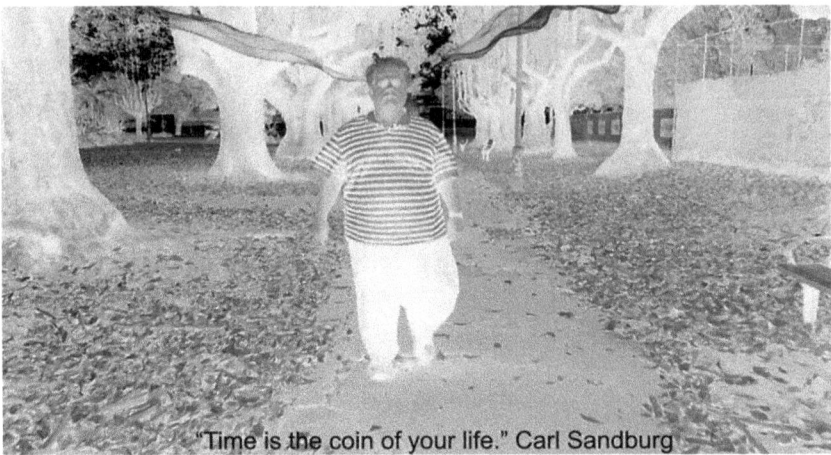

Figure 4.2: *The spiral of time* (still), John Conomos, 2013, HD video, 5 minutes duration.
Source: Courtesy of the artist.

To conclude, the self-portrait and essay film and video have been significant in my work as an artist, critic and educator. Ever since becoming a cinephile in the 1960s and 1970s, when the medium first surfaced in this country, I have been attracted to the untold experimental pliability of video. It was a huge leap of faith at that time, a gamble of sorts, to imagine the liminal horizons of this emerging art form. Despite the occasional 'moral panic'-charged critiques of this 'new' medium back then, its overall magnetic undertow of essayistic experimentation and critical thinking drew me into the aesthetic and literary/philosophical avant-garde of modernism, and cinema and the visual and performing arts allowed me as an image-maker, critic and writer to produce zig-zag connections between these disparate arts and disciplines. The essay form and the self-portrait gave me (and continue to do so, after 30 years) a compelling way to find new paths of articulation with my own life's autobiographical, existential and cultural horizons.

5

The mutable face

Michele Barker and Anna Munster

In this chapter we focus on the ways in which the neurosciences intersect with psychology and how, together with imaging technologies and techniques of identification, these come to constitute a complex, contemporary field of 'faciality'. We refer to our own work, which examines how the face and scientific imaging combine to create this shifting field. Here we explore the historical links between the early natural and medical sciences of the nineteenth century and contemporary obsessions with facial symmetry and 'genuine' facial expression found in neuropsychology and neural marketing. We draw upon the history of facial expression as it works its way through the early medical photographic images of hysterics' faces in Charles Darwin's *The expression of the emotions in man and animals*. Ideas about the face as a site for the expression of genuine and staged emotion that germinated in early neuroscience have now become part of contemporary analysis of cultural and social phenomena, such as Barak Obama's 2008 presidential campaign. In the video installation *Duchenne's smile*[1] we make these historical and contemporary links, examining emerging paradigms for how we imagine identity today at the intersection of expression, technologies and securitisation.

* * *

---

1 Michele Barker and Anna Munster, *Duchenne's smile*, two-channel video installation, 2009.

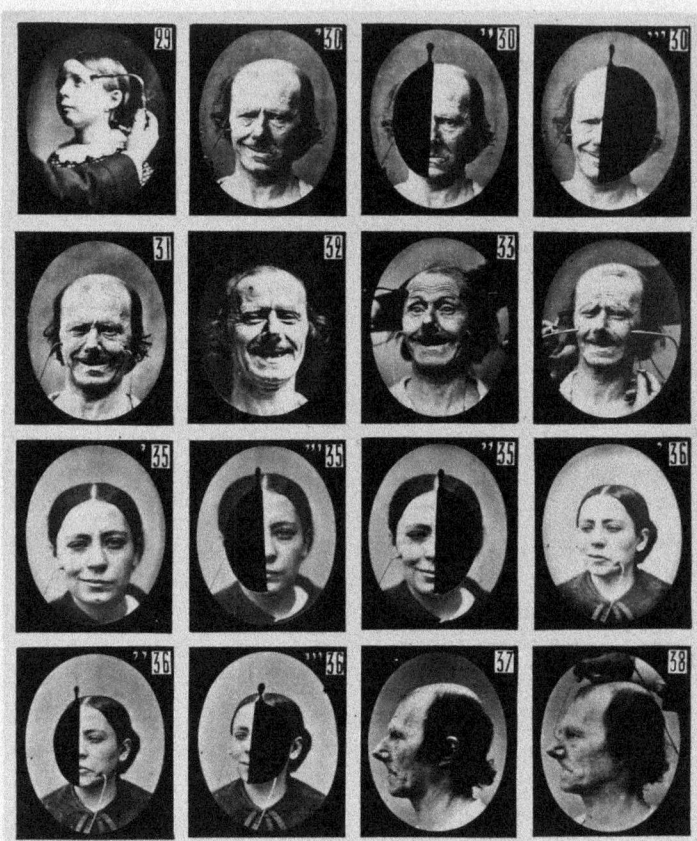

Figure 5.1: Photographic montage depicting different facial expressions induced by electrical currents.

Source: Photographs by Guillaume Duchenne de Boulogne, from *Mécanisme de la physionomie humaine, ou, analyse électro-physiologique de l'expression des passions*, 1862, copyrighted work available under Creative Commons Attribution only licence CC BY 4.0.

5. THE MUTABLE FACE

Duchenne's ultimate legacy may be that he set the stage, as it were, for Charcot's visual theater of the passions and defined the essential dramaturgy of all the visual theaters, both scientific and artistic, that have since been conceived in the attempt to picture our psyches ... In the end, Duchenne's *Mecanisme de la physionomie humaine* and the photographic stills from its experimental theater of electroshock excitations established the modern field on which the struggle to depict and thus discern the ever-elusive meanings of our coded faces continues even now to be waged.[2]

The human face is often seen, culturally and analytically, as the primary site of the expression of emotion and character, becoming the place for imaging and fixing identity. Yet identity is a complex and fickle phenomenon to capture, relying not simply upon historical norms but also technical developments, the rise of particular scientific paradigms and the relation of these to modes of visual perception. During periods of accelerated technical and scientific change, what the face 'expresses'—and hence what kind of identity resides on or behind it—is open to a number of coexisting conceptions. The face, then, is a surface, but not one that simply reveals or hides the depth of emotion or meaning. Instead, this surface is itself a complex meshing of technical and expressive histories of the measuring and organisation of emotion. The imaging of the face by specific media—such as photography, and now facial-recognition software and databases—is caught up with these histories of the face's surface, participating in and contributing to a specific regime of measurement. This regime finds its apotheosis today in technologies for imaging the face as a surface that is recognisable, expressible within tightly circumscribed patterns and, ultimately, the object and manifestation of a socio-technical formation of bioinformatic control.

This chapter examines how the imaging of the face as a site of emotion and expression drew initially on the role photography played in the development of a taxonomy of emotions in the work of Charles Darwin. It particularly traces the ways in which Darwin drew on the photographs of neurologist Guillaume-Benjamin-Amand Duchenne de Boulogne, who worked at the Salpêtrière hospital in Paris during the second half of the nineteenth century. Duchenne used electro-physiological devices wired to the faces of his subjects

---

2   RA Sobieszek, *Ghost in the shell: Photography and the human soul, 1850–2000*, Cambridge, MA, MIT Press, 2003, p. 79.

to send electrical currents that would hold facial expressions in place to match the long shutter speeds his camera required. The chapter casts light on this entanglement of expression, technics and imaging as it also discusses the authors' audiovisual artwork, *Duchenne's smile*. In this video installation, we explore the heritage and legacy of what is now known as the Duchenne smile—the staging and construction of 'genuine' expression in the genesis of neurological science and psychology via the work of Darwin, Duchenne and others—through to the contemporary capture of facial expression in face recognition software. We also discuss the shift from the imaging of the face in the earlier attempt to 'freeze' expression to a fascination with fleeting and barely seen micro-expressions that are today seen to characterise the 'truth' of the face. We argue that it is important to identify the ways in which the face continues to be redrawn as a control surface by combining with new techniques and media and in conjunction with social and political currents and movements.

In 1872, almost two decades after the publication of *On the origin of species*, Darwin's *The expression of the emotions in man and animals* was published. This work meshed Darwin's theories of evolution with what he identified as the instinctive—and universal—behaviours of human beings. In arguing for a shared human and animal ancestry via evolution, he directly questioned Charles Bell's *Anatomy and philosophy of expression*,[3] which claimed human expression to be the result of a divine musculature.

With physiognomy still widely revered, and camera-based photography in its infancy, *Expression* offered a mix of the familiar along with the novel, made possible by new imaging technologies.[4] Much has been written about Darwin's observations and his use of

---

3   Charles Bell, *Essays on the anatomy and philosophy of expression*, London, John Murray, 1824.
4   Darwin himself makes reference to the physiognomical drawings of the seventeenth-century painter Charles Le Brun. Le Brun was interested in contributing to a fledgling and pseudoscience of physiognomy in which the face could be 'read' for a range of true expressions of the passions—wonder, reverence, admiration and so on. Darwin, however, explains that he is not interested in physiognomy per se because it concentrates on expression as recognition of (underlying) character. Darwin is more interested in the relations between the movement of the facial musculature and the movement of emotions via expression across the face. He therefore sets up the possibility for a new regime of faciality, as we will begin to outline in this chapter, one that is not concerned with depth and personhood but rather with surface and a moving field of visuality discerned across the face. See Darwin, *The expression of the emotions in man and animals*, London, John Murray, 1872, pp. 1–5.

heliotype plates to create photographic reproductions to illustrate his text, for this was one of the first instances of a scientific publication being illustrated with photographs. Until the nineteenth century, scientific illustration—linocuts, woodblock, watercolours—adhered to a set of unwritten standards: the expectation was that the illustration resembled the subject matter being discussed and this confirmed the authority of both the author and the artist. According to Phillip Prodger, the introduction of photographic illustration rendered this system useless:

> Once the vision threshold was breached, new thinking was required. Photographs assumed a dual role. They illustrated something but they were also experiments in their own right. They became more than mere pictures—they became data. At that point, scientists became concerned about exactly how their photographs were made. They developed self-contained protocols to enable like-minded scholars to reproduce their results.[5]

Darwin was to find images from a variety of sources, including the Swedish photographer Oscar Rejlander, who was better known for altering and manipulating photographs than his ability to photographically illustrate a scientific treatise. A fine-art painter, Rejlander has come to be regarded as one of the first wave of art photographers, known for introducing the composite image into the photographic mainstream. Not surprisingly, Darwin's choice of Rejlander and the subsequent highly stylised images Darwin created for *Expression* would be questioned by future generations. But for Darwin, ultimately, image production was not a matter of process but rather an end result.

Nevertheless process did matter, and perhaps of greater significance here was the inclusion of images resulting from the work of neurologist Guillaume-Benjamin-Amand Duchenne de Boulogne. Duchenne was based at the Salpêtrière hospital in Paris, where he researched muscular electrophysiology—the perceived electrical dysfunction underlying neurological conditions, ranging from strokes and epilepsy through to the more questionable areas of hysteria and insanity. It was his work using electrical currents to isolate certain facial muscle groups—published in his treatise *The mechanism of human facial expression,*

---

5   Phillip Prodger, *Darwin's camera: Art and photography in the theory of evolution*, Oxford, Oxford University Press, 2009, pp. xxiii.

or an electro-physiological analysis of the expression of the passions applicable to the practice of the fine arts[6]—that came to the attention of Darwin (see Figures 5.2 and 5.3).

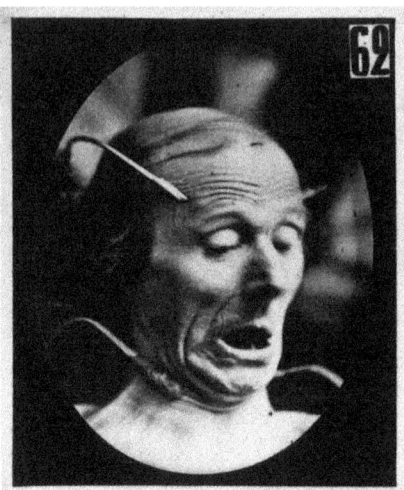 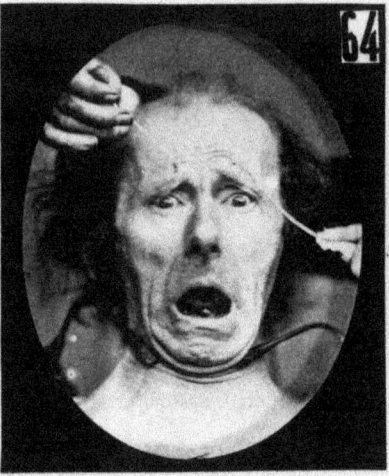

Figures 5.2 and 5.3: The facial expression of fear being induced by electrical currents.

Source: Photographs by Guillaume Duchenne de Boulogne, from *Mécanisme de la physionomie humaine, ou, analyse électro-physiologique de l'expression des passions*, 1862, copyrighted work available under Creative Commons Attribution only licence CC BY 4.0.

Darwin was deeply interested in Duchenne's work but ultimately had reservations that the extreme facial expressions produced by the neurologist's research would be misread or would require more information than was possible to provide in *Expression*. Of the few Duchenne images he did use, he requested some be redrawn—with the electrical apparatus removed from the picture. But it is precisely the relationship between Duchenne's electro-physiological devices and the resulting images that resonate the most in the contemporary context. The images appear, literally, shocking, and offer a disturbing insight into some of the experimental medical and scientific practices of the mid-nineteenth century.

---

6   Guillame-Benjamin-Amand Duchenne de Boulogne, *The mechanism of human facial expression,* trans. RA Cuthbertson, Cambridge, Cambridge University Press, 1990 [1862].

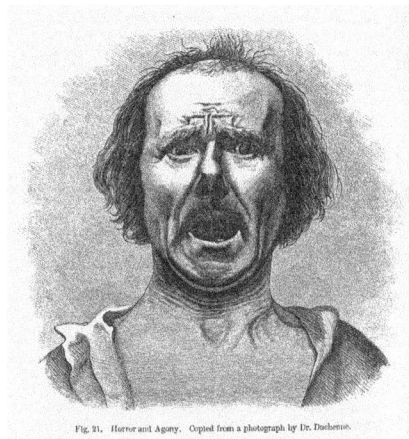 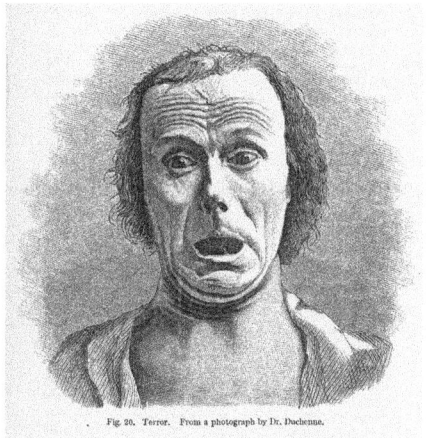

Fig. 21. Horror and Agony. Copied from a photograph by Dr. Duchenne.   Fig. 20. Terror. From a photograph by Dr. Duchenne.

Figure 5.4: Left: Horror and agony; Figure 5.5: Right: Terror.

Source: Both figures copied from photographs by Guillaume Duchenne de Boulogne, in Charles Darwin, *The expression of the emotions in man and animals*, Chapter XII, 'Surprise, Astonishment, Fear, Honour', 1872, copyrighted work available under Creative Commons Attribution only licence CC BY 4.0.

The afflictions of the inmates of the Salpêtrière made them perfect candidates for Duchenne's research and documentation: muscular paralysis and facial anaesthetics made them extremely malleable. The flow of sustained electrical currents allowed Duchenne to overcome the limits of photography's then long shutter speeds to have his sitters 'hold' a pose for an extended period. As Prodger notes:

> Instead of accelerating the photographic process to produce instantaneous images, as others had tried to do, Duchenne devised a system for freezing the activity of his subjects long enough to accommodate the lengthy exposure times.[7]

In calibrating the speeds of his subjects to the speed of the technology, Duchenne reveals a moment that moves beyond Darwin's fleeting emotions; while the expressions are undeniably involuntary, they are difficult, as Darwin discovered, to classify with any certainty. His electrical probes enabled him to isolate and control the appearance of various fluxes of emotional states yet always out of context of any real event. Although using photographs as well as illustrations gave *Expression* an air of scientific authenticity, the technical challenges of speed were yet to be overcome. Around the same time that Darwin and

---

7   Prodger, 2009, pp. 81–2.

Duchenne were considering facial expressions and how to capture them, French surgeon and physiologist Etienne-Jules Marey was attempting to record movement. In 1874, he developed the photographic gun that enabled him to take 12 frames per second. By 1882 he had successfully created what would be termed a chronophotographic fixed-plate camera, equipped with a timed shutter. Thanks to this technique he was able to combine successive images of a single movement on a single plate. By 1890 he had successfully developed a system of sequential images on transparent celluloid and an electromagnetically operated camera to display them.[8]

In the two-channel video installation *Duchenne's smile*, we explore the heritage and legacy of the Duchenne smile, from the staging and construction of 'genuine' expression in the development of nineteenth-century neurological science through to attempts to capture facial expression in contemporary face-recognition software. The installation questions whether images and the capture of 'real' facial expressions are part of a social and technical system constructing 'true' emotions. Further, it asks what affective and institutional politics arise from this typology of 'real emotions'. The work explores how this typology supports such diverse organisations and forms as police forces, public relations and marketing firms, securitisation and the media's imaging of contemporary politics.

The left channel contains tightly cropped images of Duchenne's portraits from his studies at the Salpêtrière. Beneath the images run fragments of horizontally scrolling text—specifically the elaborate chapter titles that Darwin used in *Expression*. The text format is reminiscent of the captions used in contemporary news bulletins: an unrelenting streaming of events.

---

8   For further information about this and other techniques and apparatuses constructed by Marey see Francois Dagognet, *Etienne-Jules Marey: A passion for the trace*, trans. Robert Galeta and Jeanine Herman, New York, Zone Books, 1992, pp. 106–7.

5. THE MUTABLE FACE

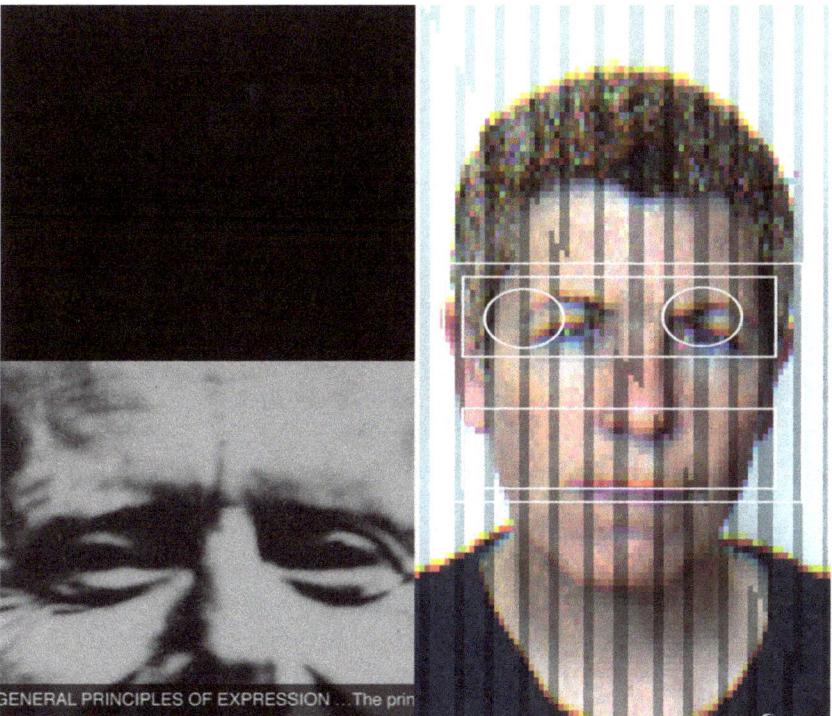

Figure 5.6: *Duchenne's smile* (still), two-channel video installation, Michele Barker and Anna Munster, 2009.
Source: Courtesy of the artists.

The right channel of the work, unhindered by the technicalities of real-time change, actively engages with the process of speed, here undermining the speed of real-time media delivery by allowing change to happen gradually over the duration of the piece. A head is framed by an almost cartoon-like vector representation of a face with ellipses for the eyes and a rectangle for the mouth. Not exactly a cartoon, it is rather the bounding boxes used in contemporary facial expression research (psychological and algorithmic) to isolate and record segments of the face. The bounding box is itself part of the contemporary regime of faciality, as it reduces the corporeality of the face to a schematic sign, which functions to include and exclude facial material for capture and further analysis. The notion of a regime of faciality rather than just a genre of portraiture is drawn from the philosophy of

Gilles Deleuze and Félix Guattari.[9] An entire regime of faciality is put in place by the connection and overlap of social, technical, aesthetic, economic, semiotic and cultural 'machines' across a specific historical or contemporary period. For Deleuze and Guattari, such machines do not have to be specifically technical; instead they operate according to a clear function that acts in conjunction with matter: 'When the faciality machine translates formed contents of whatever kind into a single substance of expression, it already subjugates them to the exclusive form of signifying and subjective expression.'[10]

Here faciality has coalesced into a machine that organises expression itself. Examples of such organisations of expression via faciality include the way in which the face of Christ organises an entire expressive religious machine of suffering, guilt and subjugation. A more contemporary example of facialisation can be found in human–computer interaction, which tends to organise computational expression around the concept of the inter*face* and, frequently, icons of smiling faces (emoticons, the start-up diagram of a face on computers and so on). Just such a facialisation machine can be seen to be operating in the diagrammatic element of the bounding box in facial-recognition software (depicted as in the right channel of *Duchenne's smile*), which attempts to organise all expressions according to its constraints. The regime to which this box belongs is a contemporary one, in which identity is mapped, controlled and expressed bioinformatically. Digital information in this way functions to express a biopolitics that is played out across the surface of the face, and through which the face becomes *the* dominant surface for tracking, tracing and controlling the subject.

Does continuity or rupture best describe the relations between contemporary regimes of faciality and those of the nineteenth century? What do we inherit from Duchenne and Darwin, and what has changed in our new facial regimes? For it is not as if one vast regime of faciality spans all history. Rather, what is important is the way in which the diagram of the face is always combining differently with new techniques and technologies and in conjunction with a socio-technical

---

9   Gilles Deleuze and Félix Guattari, *A thousand plateaus*, trans. Brian Massumi, Minneapolis, University of Minnesota Press, 2005, pp. 176–85.
10 Deleuze and Guattari, 2005, pp. 179–80. For an extended discussion and critique of faciality in interface design, see Anna Munster, *Materializing new media: Embodiment in information aesthetics*, Hanover, NH, Dartmouth College Press, 2006, pp. 117–49.

machine. In the wake of 9/11, securitisation measures, taken by the US government especially, have exploded around biometric research and development. These have been deployed in facial-recognition software and retina scanning at airports and in voice analysis of recordings of actual and potential terrorist suspects.[11] One can easily see how such technologies share a lineage with the profiling of human types that began with the criminological sciences of the nineteenth century and their deployment of anthropometrical and physiognomical techniques to produce fixed facial and corporeal identities. As Michel Foucault had already suggested in 1978 for a range of biopolitical forms of control, first emerging in the eighteenth century, these were techniques for the management and governance of the entire life of the human.[12] Darwin's systematisation of human emotions via a taxonomy that relied upon fixed facial expression recorded photographically seems commensurate with this biopolitical project.

The installation *Duchenne's smile* is a visual response to these issues of continuity and rupture, indicated especially in the right video channel as the subject's face is gradually pixellated and overlaid with bounding box elements, which are similar to those used in facial-recognition software. Pixellation of the subject's face in the right channel over time makes the viewer aware of a digital aesthetic at work, which has become so ubiquitous as to be almost naturalised in contemporary forms of portraiture. By foregrounding the encoding that is taking place, the installation raises questions about not just the authentic smile but also the authentic face. Any semblance of the indexical that may have occurred in Duchenne's portraits has ceased to exist in the contemporary example of portraiture that is the installation *Duchenne's smile*.

It is also the case that certain branches of contemporary psychology that use techniques for capturing and interpreting facial expression also construct certain continuities with Darwin. The evolutionary psychologist Paul Ekman has styled himself as the successor to Darwin's project of expressing emotions in 'man and the animal'. Paul Ekman and Warren Friesen's late 1960s research examined 'micro-

---

11 For example, see Adam Peneberg, 'The surveillance society', *Wired Magazine* online, 2001, www.wired.com/2001/12/surveillance/.
12 Foucault's lecture series of 1978 given at the Collège de France signal these preoccupations. The English translation of these has only been recently published. See Michel Foucault, *Security, Territory, Population*, London, Palgrave, 2007, p. 16.

expressions', which built on psychotherapeutic work undertaken in that decade. Facial and bodily movements ordinarily imperceptible to the human eye were observed through frame-by-frame scanning of video recordings of therapeutic sessions: 'Micro displays may be fragments of a squelched, neutralized or masked display.'[13] According to Ekman and Friesen, if you were able to see or train yourself to see at the rate of video recording—1/25th of a second—you could observe a micro-expression. Importantly, they argued that these betrayed both 'real emotion'—the truth of what someone was feeling—*and* attempts to mask or deceive the observing eye. One would expect the keen observer, on the other hand, to receive contradictory information from facial cues: simulated messages, micro-leakage of information contradicting simulations, and such deception clues as squelched displays and improperly performed simulations.[14]

In the 1970s, Ekman and Friesen developed the Facial Action Coding System (FACS).[15] This is an instructional set of techniques for categorising facial expression based on the groups of facial muscles that produce the expressions, and which they called 'Action Units'. Then they developed FACS AID, a database that facilitates the relational linking of facial expressions to their psychological interpretations. Ekman further consolidated the connection between micro-expressions and the FACs system, relating the involuntary micro-movements of facial muscles such as we see in the Duchenne smile with the display of 'trustworthy' emotional displays, on the one hand, and *voluntary* micro- and macro-movements across the face with a person's potential to mask emotion and deceive an observer, on the other.

> When emotional expressions lack a muscular movement that is difficult to make voluntarily, that expression should be less reliable; and those expressions that contain the reliable muscle should be more likely to be trustworthy.[16]

---

13   Paul Ekman and Wallace V Friesen, 'Nonverbal leakage and clues to deception', *Psychiatry*, vol. 32, no. 1, 1969, p. 89.
14   Ekman and Friesen, 1969, pp. 98–9.
15   For further information on FACS see the website Dataface, maintained by Ekman and Friesen, face-and-emotion.com/dataface/facs/description.jsp.
16   Paul Ekman, 'Darwin, deception, and facial expression', *Annals of the New York Academy of Sciences*, 1000, 2003, pp. 205–21.

There are two important points to draw from Ekman and the late twentieth-century contribution to contemporary regimes of imaging, interpreting and organising the face as a surface of expression. First, in order to observe human emotion on the face at its most expressive and most genuine, the observer must calibrate their vision to the temporality of media technologies. We have, then, replaced human vision with what Paul Virilio calls machine vision.[17] Second, although the machine vision of video recording reveals micro-expressions, the micro-expression itself both reveals and masks; it is capable of supplying truth and deception simultaneously. Only by ongoing training and the calibration of human vision to the speeds of machine vision is the expert observer able to make the call between one and the other. Hence a new regime of faciality emerges in which the moving image and the face come to organise a relation to truth, to the subject being observed and to the observer. It is these relations that organise contemporary surveillance, and so much more insidiously than simple surveillance, even if the latter is now ubiquitous.

The constant fluctuations between truth and deception in this new regime of facialisation provide the drama and indeed atmosphere of the television series *Lie to me*.[18] The character of Cal Lightman, who heads up The Lightman Group corporation in the series, is loosely modeled on Ekman and his Ekman Group. Just like Ekman's corporation, The Lightman Group's employees are deployed by law enforcement agencies to solve crimes from homicide to terrorism. Using techniques based on FACS and technologies such as voice analysis to 'catch' and read micro-expression, Cal and his employees calibrate their observations to the real time of media and computational biometric technologies. But this calibration means that they are constantly subjecting everything—including each other's facial expressions—to these techniques. In a regime in which micro-expressivity assumes primacy, both truth and deception become intra- and intersubjectively interchangeable. What *Lie to me* both captures and engenders in its constant search for both truth and deception across the face is the broad atmosphere of suspicion that permeates contemporary societies

---

17   Paul Virilio, *War and cinema*, London, Verso Books, 1988.
18   The series was created by Samuel Baum and originally aired on Fox Television between 2009 and 2011.

governed by these new methods of control and securitisation: societies in which, potentially, 'Anyone can be presumed to be a candidate for insider threat', as put by US Department of Homeland Security.[19]

Crucially, what has changed for the contemporary facial regime that both images and interprets the human subject is that we are not simply dealing with a ramping up of techniques of governance derived from the nineteenth century. The human is now not simply to be subjected to techniques of management but itself becomes a technique via its enmeshing with technologies of the moving image. This human is a category that functions as a technique for managing a broader scoping out of the contemporary technosocial scape:

> Human eyes are capable of high-resolution, stereo-optical vision with immense range, and, integrated with a highly plastic brain, make humans uniquely capable of discovery, integration, and complex pattern recognition. Human hands constitute a dexterous, sensitive biomechanical system that, integrated with the brains and eyes, are unmatched by current and near-future robotic technologies. Humans operate in groups synergistically and dynamically, adjusting perceptions, relationships and connections as needed on a real-time and virtually instantaneous basis. Human language capabilities exist and operate within a dimensional space that is far more complex and fluid than any known artificial architectures.[20]

We see such a scoping-out emerging in the 2004 National Plan for Research and Development in Support of Critical Infrastructure Protection. This plan amounts to techniques and strategies for producing what are called the 'Common Operating Picture for Critical Infrastructure'. This picture is produced by 'sensing out' deceptive behaviours at the micro or molecular level in persons who are equally deemed trustworthy and threatening.

The picture or image produced in the contemporary moment is not, then, the profile of an individual or even a type of human being with circumscribed characters and behaviours, as it was especially at the height of nineteenth-century anthropology, criminology and psychology. That is, when Darwin was writing and Duchenne taking

---

19 Department of Homeland Security Science and Technology Directorate, *The national plan for research and development in support of critical infrastructure protection*, 2004, p. 43, www.dhs.gov/xlibrary/assets/ST_2004_NCIP_RD_PlanFINALApr05.pdf.
20 Department of Homeland Security, 2004, p. 63.

photographs. Instead, we are now dealing with a completely abstracted yet highly technical image—an abstract machine of faciality—that must be constantly subjected to attenuation and calibration so as to maintain operability. Humans are only part of this picture and, now lacking determined character and specific intention, the profiler and profiled become interchangeable. Distinctions made at the level of intention, character and action are ultimately of little importance for such a bioinformatic regime. This is why catching the 'wrong suspect' is not something that requires explanation but can be passed off as a mere 'system' error. This is increasingly played out through systems of recognition in high-risk arenas such as airports. In 2009, for example, a Californian student, Nicholas George, was randomly singled out at Pomona airport for questioning by Transportation Security Administration (TSA) officers:

> George had been singled out by behavior-detection officers: TSA screeners trained to pick out suspicious or anomalous behavior in passengers. There are about 3,000 of these officers working at some 161 airports across the United States, all part of a four-year-old program called Screening Passengers by Observation Technique (SPOT), which is designed to identify people who could pose a threat to airline passengers.
>
> It remains unclear what the officers found anomalous about George's behavior, and why he was detained ... But the incident has brought renewed attention to a burgeoning controversy: is it possible to know whether people are being deceptive, or planning hostile acts, just by observing them?[21]

Let us return, then, to the question of whether the face today is a surface whose identity can be traced back to the taxonomy of expression and emotion that Darwin initiated in 1872. We have suggested that contemporary bioinformatic regimes for drawing out the face as a fluctuating surface of micro-expressions, especially via the codification system designed by Ekman and Friesan, extends the Darwinian trajectory for locating truth and identity in the face. Importantly, the enmeshing of media technologies—initially photography but now facial-recognition software—with a science of facial expression shows how we are not dealing simply with the human face but rather

---

21   Sharon Wienberger, 'Airport security: Intent to deceive?', *Scientific American*, 26 May 2010, www.scientificamerican.com/article.cfm?id=airport-security-intent-to-deceive.

a machine of facialisation. We have also suggested, however, that such a machine only makes sense, indeed is itself expressive, through its relations with social and political machines. Today we are in the grip of a face whose identity has been entirely abstracted from and by the technical speeds *and* the biopolitics in which it participates. What matters in this new regime are issues of signal, distortion and clarity and what measures, techniques and technologies are to be devised and deployed to produce this common operating picture. The common operating picture to be discovered in the face today is precisely the operation of the (moving) picture.

6
BarkTV: Portrait of an innovator

Jennifer Deger

I

In his book *Multiple arts*, Jean-Luc Nancy describes the portrait as 'first and foremost an encounter', though in fact, as Nancy clearly appreciates, the art of portraiture puts multiple encounters into play.[1] The most obvious is that between the viewer and the subject of the artwork, an experience often charged with an unnerving immediacy.

Yet all portraits await viewers already imprinted with the echo of encounter. More than most, this is an art form that calls attention to the relationship between artist and subject: two people united in a shared project of portrayal. It is into this prefigured relationship that the viewer enters, assuming the vantage point of an artist who never completely vacates their place. Nancy describes this effect as the artist occupying the foreground of the canvas. From here, the viewer faces the figure before them: another being presenting themselves for encounter.

---

1   Jen-Luc Nancy, *Multiple arts*, Stanford, Stanford University Press, 2006.

As these dynamic relations structure portraiture (even, I would suggest, when the face does not look directly out, or when there is no face at all), it becomes an art without objects, only subjects. Herein lies a strangely unsettling source of their allure: portraits seem to offer some kind of direct experiential encounter with an other even though there can be no mistaking the work of mediation involved.

For Nancy, though, portraiture's most compelling, and defining, encounter occurs elsewhere: namely, between the depicted figure and themselves. Portraits, after all, concern something more, something deeper, than merely a figure posed for public view. The portrait artist's true purpose is neither mutuality, nor resemblance. It is character: that complex inner tangle of qualities that mark individuals as at once unique and yet deeply, and recognisably, human.[2] And so Nancy identifies the portrait as an art concerned with the 'extraction' of character, as artists work the tremulous surface of the subject in pursuit of an inner but somehow indelible relationship between a self and itself. Character in this reckoning exceeds what someone might be comfortable with—or capable of—publicly portraying to others. For Nancy what is at stake in portraiture is the depiction of a 'singular trait of an *intimate disunion*'.[3] From this perspective, the work of portraiture involves a breaking past the veneer of self-presentation in order to reveal the fundamental disunity of the self. This becomes portraiture's defining point of tension. This is where the life lies.

Nancy puts it this way: '"Art" is the name of this fragile other encounter.'[4]

---

2   As Marcia Pointon points out, it is only since the Renaissance that portraiture has been expected to reveal character along with status and identity: '[F]rom the Renaissance to our own day, portraiture carries a huge burden of expectation: a process of comparing and matching takes place as viewers (guided by curators and media commentators) construct an empathetic narrative based on fragments of data from a life set alongside the portrait image, the one illuminating the other.' Marcia Pointon, *Portrayal and the search for identity,* London, Reaktion, 2012, p. 15.
3   Nancy, 2006, p. 246, emphasis added.
4   Nancy, 2006. Of course ethnography has likewise been defined in terms of encounter. See for instance Michael Jackson, *Minima ethnographica: Intersubjectivity and the anthropological project*, Chicago, University of Chicago Press, 1998; and Franca Tamisari, 'Body, vision and movement: In the footprints of the ancestors', *Oceania*, vol. 68, no. 4, 1998, pp. 249–70.

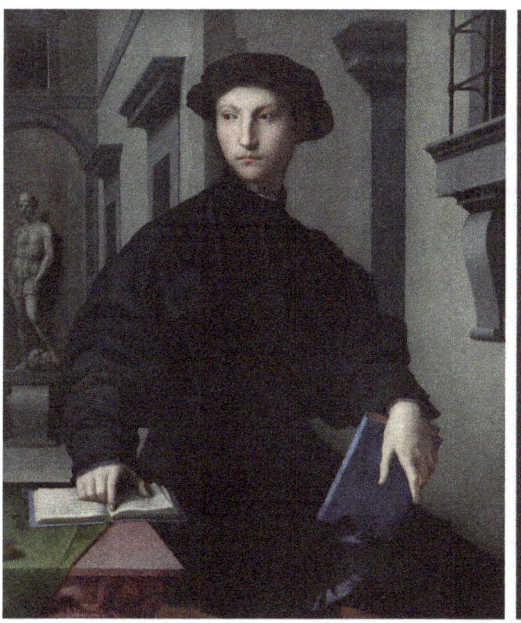 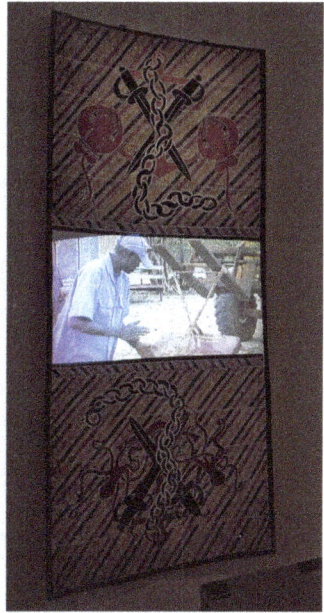

Figure 6.1: Left: *Portrait of Ugolino Martelli,* Angelo Bronzino, 1536 or 1537, oil on wood, oil on poplar wood.
Source: Wikimedia Commons.

Figure 6.2: Right: *Djalkiri #1*, David Bukulatjpi, Jennifer Deger and Marrawakamirr Marrawungu, 2009, video and acrylic on bark.
Source: Courtesy of the artists.

II

This essay is an attempt to flesh out the possibilities of encounter engendered by a mixed-media artwork that my collaborators and I labelled *Djalkiri #1*, but is nicknamed the BarkTV.[5] I present it here,

---

5   This is by no means an unprecedented argument. See Melinda Hinkson, 'Seeing more than black and white: Picturing Aboriginality at Australia's National Portrait Gallery', *Australian Humanities Review*, vol. 49, 2010, pp. 5–28, who claims certain Aboriginal painting styles as portraiture as a means of disrupting the normative vision of cultural institutions such as the National Portrait Gallery. John von Sturmer, on the other hand, has dismissed the suggestion that bark paintings are portraits. See John von Sturmer, 'A limping world: Works in the Arnott's collection—some conceptual underpinnings', in *They are meditating: Bark paintings from the MCA's Arnott's Collection*, Sydney, Museum of Contemporary Art, 2008, pp. 35–53. In exploring this argument here I am concerned with activating the relationship between images and other images as much as the relationship between image and stories that are more usually offered in the exegesis of Aboriginal art.

in the context of a collection of responses to digital portraiture, with conflicting impulses. Claiming *Djalkiri #1* as portrait feels immediately constraining, if not downright colonising. If, as art historian Marcia Pointon argues, portraiture is one of the 'great defining metaphors of Western culture',[6] then why impose the category at all? What might be gained? What will be obscured, obliterated even, in the process?

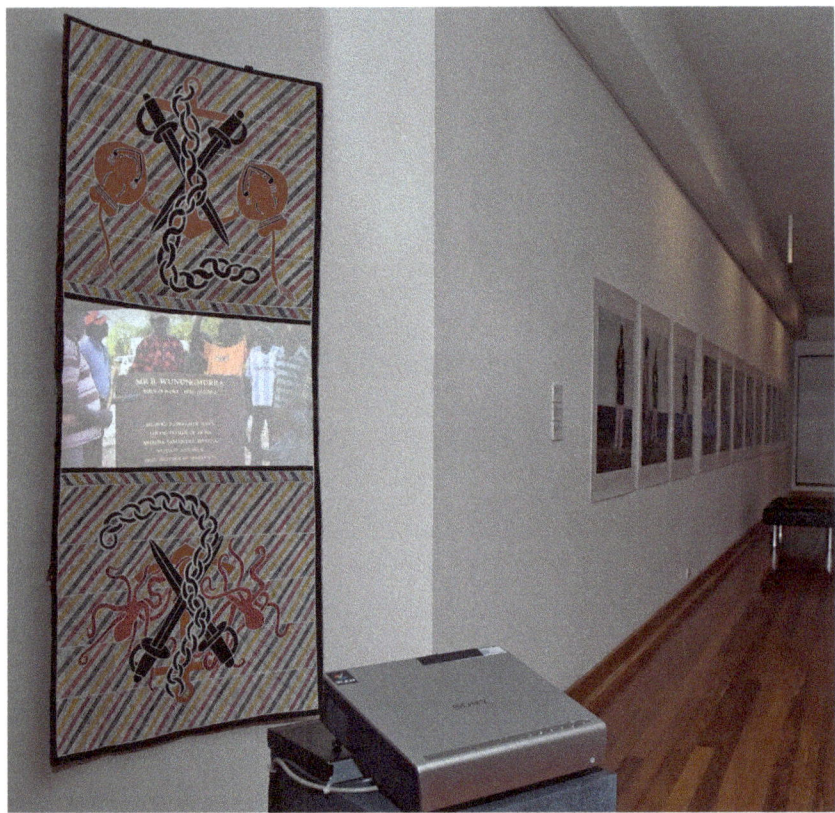

Figure 6.3: *Djalkiri #1*, Macquarie University Art Gallery, December 2009.
Source: Courtesy of the artists.

Certainly from a purely formal perspective, there is no obvious resemblance between our BarkTV and, for example, Bronzino's delicate masterpiece *Portrait of Ugolino Martelli*, a work I first came to know through my reading of Nancy.[7] Yet the more I think about this kind of

---

6   Pointon, 2012, p. 26.
7   I choose to use it here, though, because I especially like the way it sits beside our bark work. I am surprised how they seem, somehow, strangely akin.

art, the more I realise that portrait artists and the Aboriginal people of Arnhem Land do share common concerns, most particularly with the art of discerning—and creatively bringing to light—the inner qualities of a person. Cultivating particular ways of seeing, both bring creative energy to the work of rendering visible distinctive marks of character; driven by revelatory purpose, both seek to manifest visible forms of likeness that tap into a power exceeding that of literal resemblance.

And so I begin with a tentative conclusion that there is something to be gained—maybe even something to be seen anew?—by approaching *Djalkiri #1* as if it is a portrait.

III

On first encountering *Djalkiri #1* the sound might be the first thing that hits you, an energetic urgency of men's ritual song punctuated by the striking of steel on steel. Or maybe, as it was for me when we flipped the 'on' switch for the first time, it will be the glow of the striated surface that catches your eye, the way the images seem to emanate from within the bark itself. Or maybe, you will be drawn closer for a second look by the force of sheer novelty.

Far less likely is that you, my imaginary art gallery visitor, will approach this multimedia installation because of its appeal as a portrait, for this is simply not the way the work appears to present itself. Where is the face? The figure? The person?

Instead, what you will encounter is a long, vertical, three-panelled bark painting, its middle section filled with a looped video projection. The sound comes from speakers built into the projector. It shouldn't take long to work out that this is an Aboriginal headstone-laying ceremony. The nine-and-a-half minute single-take video shows a forklift being used to slowly lift and position the stone while men sing to the beat of clap sticks. The man in an orange T-shirt leading the ritual uses the bottom end of a shifting spanner to strike the steel blade of a tomahawk held above his head. This use of tools as practical instruments—in every sense of the word—is one of the aspects of the work much remarked upon by gallery visitors.

The top and bottom panels feature octopuses and stingrays darting beside long-bladed knives rakishly crossed over a heavy-chained anchor, the in-between spaces backfilled with ochre-coloured cross-hatching. It's a dance of intertwinement that confounds conventional expectations regarding the traditional stuff of Indigenous material culture. In fact, if you look closely you might notice that the paint on the top and bottom panels is acrylic rather than ochre, ochre remaining de rigueur for barks produced for sale in the fine art market.

The video itself is observational in style—traditionally ethnographic, one might say. The camera quietly moves across the scene following the unfolding events. I shot it myself and use it here with permissions from both the relevant Dhalwangu clan leaders and the orange-shirted *djungaya* (ritual manager).

It would be a mistake to see these elements as either evidence of a playful cultural hybridity or an example of the degeneration of traditional forms. As each one of the men and women in this video would tell you, this is Yolngu *rom* (law, culture, ancestral precedent). The anchor and the knives and the sea creatures belong together, as do the grader and the shifting spanner, and by extension the bark and the video. Any explanation as to why this is the case, however, would likely be brief and guarded. Some say these images are the result of the history of exchange between Yolngu and Macassan fishermen. Others insist that it is really about relations between Yolngu and Balanda (non-Aboriginal, white people). But all agree that the incorporation of ostensibly foreign material culture has deep ancestral significance.[8] The objects depicted relate to the activities of Birrinydji, the ancestral sea captain, blacksmith and swordsman who sailed across Arnhem Land, dropping anchor at several places, including the Dhalwangu homeland of Gurrumurru.[9] Stories associated with Birrinydji and the origins of Yolngu ownership and mastery of 'foreign technologies' are *dhuyu* (sacred, restricted and dangerous) among my friends and

---

8   For an analysis and elaboration of what he calls the 'Birrinydji legacy' given to him by Warramirri clan leaders on neighbouring Elcho Island, see Ian McIntosh, 'The iron furnace of Birrinydji', in Alan Rumsey and James Weiner (eds), *Mining and Indigenous lifeworlds in Australia and Papua New Guinea*, Oxon, Sean Kingston Publishing, 2004, pp. 12–30.

9   Some Yolngu and some anthropologists have suggested that because of their associations with Birrinydji, Yirritja clans—or perhaps certain Yirritja clans—are directly associated with innovation and technological incorporation, while those from the opposite moiety, Dhuwa, are inherently more conservative. My own Yolngu collaborators are reluctant to make such distinctions.

colleagues. But at any Dhalwangu funeral you will encounter people singing and dancing foundational events involving such items as knives, steel axes, telescopes, cloth and tobacco.

IV

'The ancestral' is hardly an adequate term to describe the sources of the ongoing and often highly reflexive dynamics of becoming in Yolngu life—and death—including, increasingly, digital practices. But it offers a place to begin. For now, perhaps the most important thing to say is that just as ancestral form and power inhere in country, sacred objects and painted designs, they also materially manifest in people themselves, through physical characteristics and even ways of thinking: ancestral identities emerge and become visible in the breadth of a nose, the tenor of a voice or the brilliance of an idea.

V

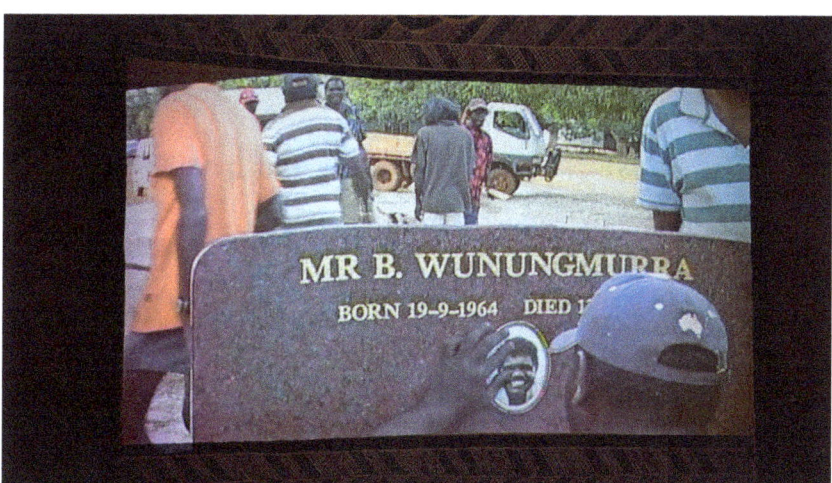

Figure 6.4: *Djalkiri #1* (detail).
Source: Courtesy of the artists.

In the final 20 seconds of the video, the headstone ceremony reaches its conclusion as a photograph of a smiling man is carefully glued into position. From the dates in gold lettering, we can calculate that he died aged 37. But we don't know his name. In keeping with current Yolngu conventions it is withheld, indicated only by the initial B.[10] For me, this is the crucial moment, the point at which the multiple media coalesce. For although his face is only glimpsed briefly at the end of the video—and then only in a photograph—there is indeed a central human figure around which it is structured and organised, a figure who is animated, called forth and made visible.

Created, at my instigation—with his wife, daughter and nephew—to be exhibited in a Sydney art gallery among other artworks by anthropologists whose lives have also become densely interwoven with their research subjects, the work acts as a performative homage to the man who became the central and defining figure in my anthropological research in Arnhem Land; a man who, by adopting me, instructing me and working alongside me as a video-maker, profoundly determined the way that Yolngu continue to see me, as much as the way I see them.[11]

---

10   I have written elsewhere at some length about the shift in Yolngu relations to images of the dead. See Jennifer Deger, *Shimmering screens: Making media in an Aboriginal community*, Minneapolis, University of Minnesota Press, 2006; and Jennifer Deger, 'Imprinting on the heart: Photography and contemporary Yolngu mournings, *Visual Anthropology*, vol. 21, no. 4, pp. 292–309.

11   As I wrote for the catalogue at the time:

interventions explores what might happen when researchers, instead of writing about their subjects, take up visual and other media as a way of relating with others. The exhibition claims the possibility of Aboriginal people working creatively with ethnographers to generate new forms and styles of cultural production. Compelled by the idea that making—and viewing—art is a critical and productive form of social engagement, *interventions* offers new ways of taking up, and taking seriously, Aboriginal ways of seeing the world.

... this exhibition is not aiming at the fine art market ... There are other kinds of economies, other kinds of exchanges at play here. By breaching conventional separations between art practice and scholarship—not to mention between the Indigenous subject and the non-Indigenous researcher—*interventions* locates artists and ethnographers in shared fields of experimentation.

Jennifer Deger, 'Making interventions', *Interventions: Experiments between art and ethnography*, Macquarie University, Sydney, 2009, pp. 1–9.

VI

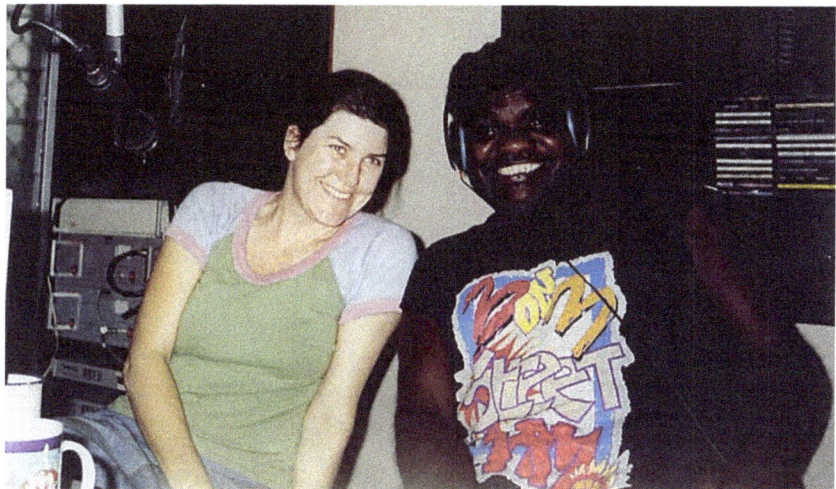

Figure 6.5: Jennifer Deger and Bangana Wunungmurra in the BRACS radio studio, Gapuwiyak 1999.
Source: Jennifer Deger.

I first met Bangana in 1994. He walked into the local community radio station where I was volunteering and announced that he wanted to work there with me. We could, he said, use the technology to strengthen Yolngu culture. Over the next few years, Bangana became my closest Yolngu friend and colleague. He oversaw the insertion of locally recorded *manikay* (clan songs) and *raypirri* (instructional messages) into a radio playlist that had previously been filled only with local favourites like ABBA, Smokey, Yothu Yindi, Kenny Rogers and Boney M. We made videos together in SuperVHS, working across northeast Arnhem Land with clan leaders and visiting film crews. He directed. I produced. We translated together.[12]

Looking back over the years since he died, I'm surprised to realise just how many of my films and artworks feature Bangana's image, often incorporating the same photograph. There are many reasons for this: his image summons up his family's identity, our relationships, and by extension my relationship with his family and community;

---

12   This essay forms a couplet with another piece about the making of this work. See Jennifer Deger, 'Constellations of us: Backstories to a bark TV', *Journal of Australian Studies*, vol. 35, no. 2, 2011, pp. 219–34.

it allows us to harness his authority and creative force as a powerful Dhalwangu man; it gestures to an enduring sense of shared loss, a specific set of stories and feelings that have become associated with him over the years. It also locates him as somehow seminal to the unfolding potentialities brought by new generations of digital media; and, of course, as foundational to the self that I have become.

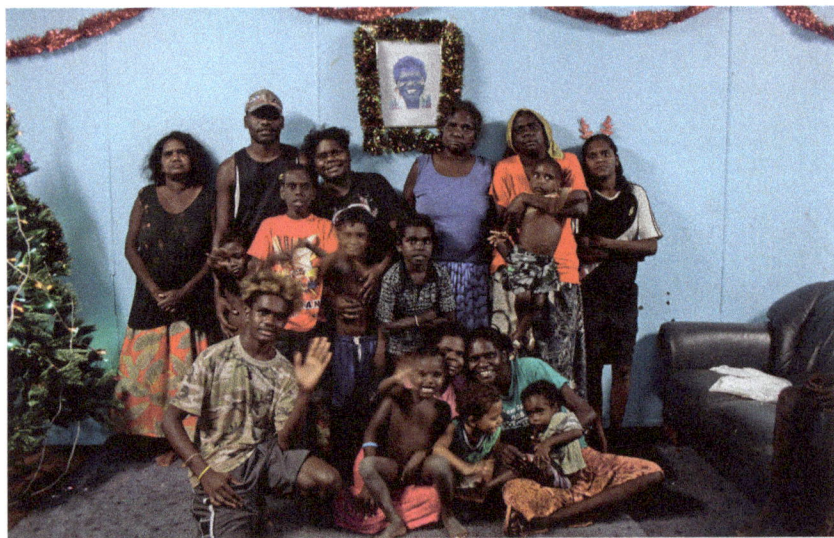

Figure 6.6: *Family portrait #3, Christmas Birrimbirr* (Christmas spirit), installation, Miyarrka Media, 2011.
Source: Courtesy of Miyarrka Media.

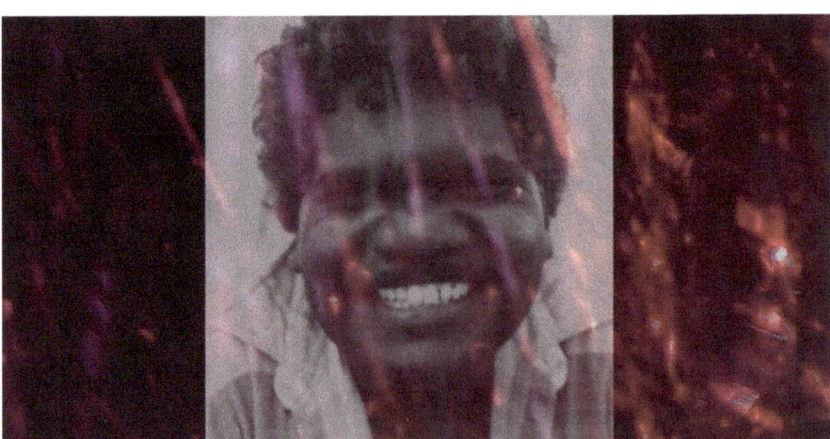

Figure 6.7: *Christmas with Wawa* (still), Jennifer Deger with Susan Marrawakamirr Marrawungu, 2007.
Source: Jennifer Deger.

VII

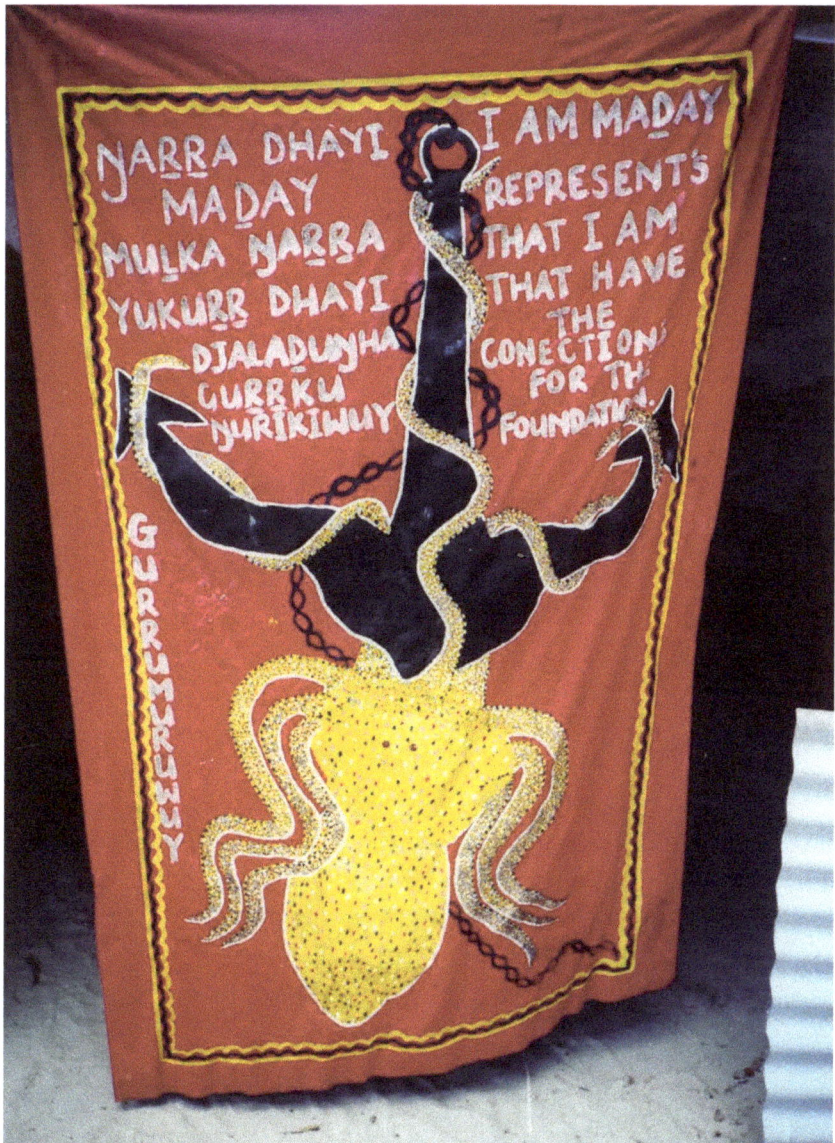

Figure 6.8: The entrance to Bangana Wunungmurra's funeral shade, 2001.

A painted cloth hung at the entrance to the shelter where we held Bangana for two weeks of ritual in the area known as *Djalkiri*. Amid the field of multicoloured dots on the body of the octopus are two slightly larger ones. These are the eyes.

Source: Jennifer Deger.

IMAGING IDENTITY

In the months and years after Bangana's death we would sometimes get spooked when we heard an unexpected clank of steel or saw shadows in the trees that looked like wriggling octopus tentacles. In hushed voices, people would tell me how at night the octopus changes colour, depending on its mood.

VIII

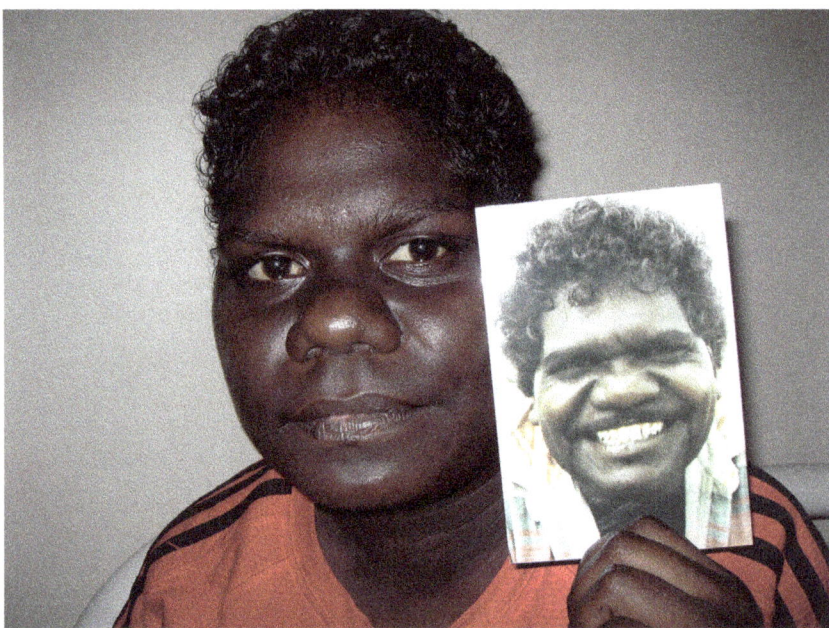

Figure 6.9: Portrait of father and daughter, 2005.

During the months after his death, Bangana's youngest daughter, Lay'pu, made a series of photographs with me, using my digital camera, showing her holding her father's image. We kept going until we got it right. She wanted to capture the likeness, to show their unmistakable connection. I've lost the one where she smiles, the one we both loved, the one shuddering with uncanny likeness.

Source: Jennifer Deger.

IX

Djalkiri is a Yolngu word for foot or footstep, but in a deeper sense it is used to refer to the underlying foundations of Yolngu life. It is the name given to the house where Bangana Wunungmurra once lived and where he is now buried, next to the shady area under the mango tree where his father held ceremonies in the early mission days of the 1970s. For those of us involved in this project, *djalkiri* means home and belonging, family and foundation, a shared history and a particular point of attachment.

Susan Marrawakamirr Marrawungu, widow of Bangana, her nephew David Bukulatjpi, and I called our work *Djalkiri #1* for all these reasons.

X

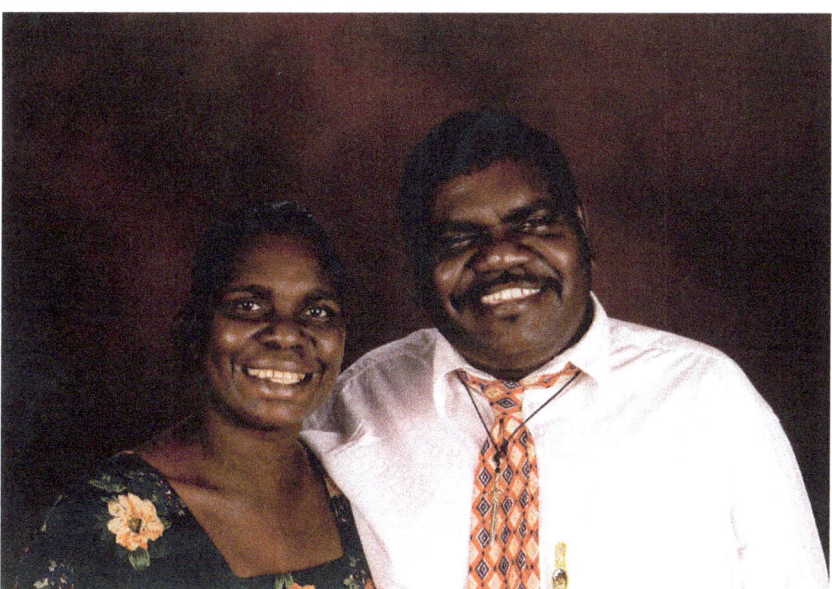

Figure 6.10: Studio portrait of Susan Marrawakamirr Marrawungu and Bangana Wunungmurra, 1997.

Bangana has arranged himself for the camera as loving family man and successful intercultural figure (complete with accidental coffee stain). He's just spoken at his first international conference, a symposium on Indigenous people in an interconnected world.

Source: Jennifer Deger.

In the above image, against the elongated diamonds and colours of his tie hangs a miniature sword, its placement foregrounding not only a Dhalwangu identity but a foundational source of power, force and ferocity. At the Dhalwangu homeland of Gurrumurru, the ancestral swordsman called Birrinydji stands with his knives crossed. Bangana's father was named after that knife. As Yolngu say, his name is on that knife— Lawarrwarkk; it also means stingray.

There's a special ritual sound for that knife. In *Djalkiri #1* we hear it when the ritual leader hits his steel tools above his head (it doesn't matter what steel is actually used). Men sing that sound too: *Ngarrk yarrk*. *Ngarrk yarrk*. In the gallery it rings out: voices, clap sticks, hands and steel in unison.

As Bangana's brother-in-law explained, an imagistic poetics not simply of place but also of emplacement unfolds as the video loops across the bark:

> The *yiki* (knife) clears the ground in preparation: the grader, the backhoe any blade can be used … With the *yiki* they clear the ground to lay the anchor. That's the foundation: the anchor, the footprint. That heavy anchor (the headstone) is going to be stamped in, stamped in forever. They're putting down the anchor, this is where he's going to stop.

XI

Anthropologists often use the term 'ancestral power' to identify both the source and subject of Yolngu creativity. We describe the ways that individuals identify themselves based on clan affiliations and complex genealogies. The difficulty with these formulations is that they suggest that Yolngu art and ritual depend entirely on the creative actions of those who came before. This obscures the degree to which this is a two-way street—the way that contemporary innovation is necessary to enliven both current generations and the ancestral.

Such work, however, is not without its risks.

When Bangana died unexpectedly from a heart attack in 2002, Marrawakamirr, Bangana's widow, and his children were in no doubt that the cause of his death was malicious sorcery, and that he was killed because he had exhibited a lethal combination of charisma, talent and wilful genius.[13] The only question was who, exactly, to

---

13 See Deger, 2006, 2011.

blame. Over the years versions of the story have continued to shift and change according to how lives have unfolded, drawing in retrospective insights and changing familial alliances. What hasn't altered is the degree to which they claim he was murdered because of who he was: a brilliant and provocative man, capable and knowledgeable in both men's business and whitefella bureaucracies, an innovative and politically nimble intercultural broker, destined, we had all thought, to lead his community through the difficult times ahead.

Designing his headstone, Marrawakamirr dug out a slightly worn and faded photograph—her favourite because of the look and the smile. She instructed me to boost the colours on the computer and then have the photograph framed in gold and mounted on a red stone, the colour of the Dhalwangu flag. This was a radical move; it was the first headstone in Gapuwiyak ever to feature a photograph. Ten years on it remains the only one.

Bangana had died at a moment of dramatic change in how Yolngu treated photographs of the dead. Until that time it had been standard practice to destroy, or at least hide away, photographs of deceased family members. For me, Bangana's funeral marked the beginning of a different attitude, where photographs might be incorporated into funerals and grieving processes, as, for example, in displaying Bangana's photograph with the coffin. But the act of putting his photo on his headstone pushed things further than I had ever seen before. It performatively claimed his role as a man of 'modern technologies', as he used to describe himself.

And so in death, as in life, Bangana assumed the stance of leader and innovator: fearless, singular and Dhalwangu. His grave became a favoured site for family portraits.

IMAGING IDENTITY

XII

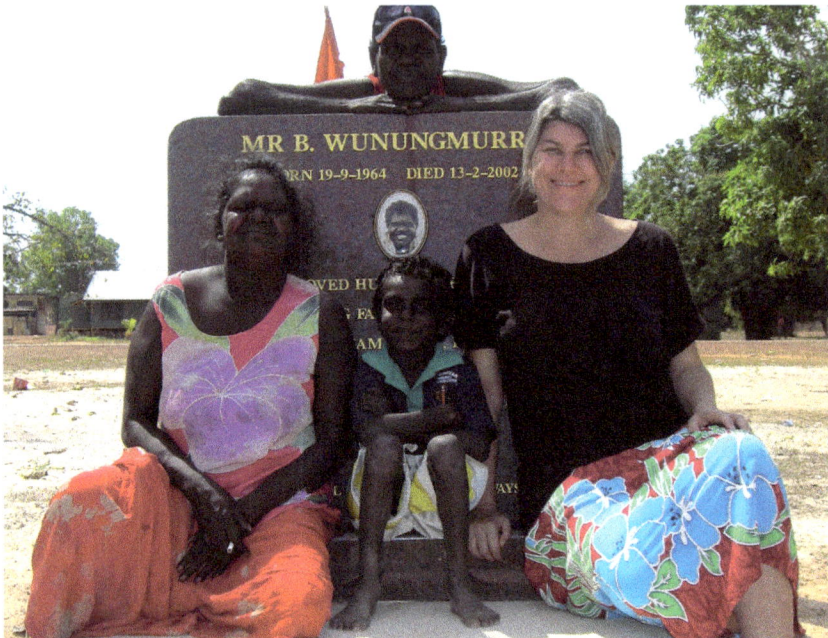

Figure 6.11: Family portrait at grave, 2007.

Source: Jennifer Deger.

I remember trying to deliberately echo Bangana's expression when we took this shot, moved by the relentless good cheer of his image. But on re-encountering my slightly too-bright smile I feel ashamed. What I see here is another moment of an ethnographic clumsiness, a failure to master this subgenre of Yolngu portraiture and self-presentation. I cannot see past my anxiety in the face of the camera. Am I imagining it, or do the others' expressions come from somewhere deeper within?

XIII

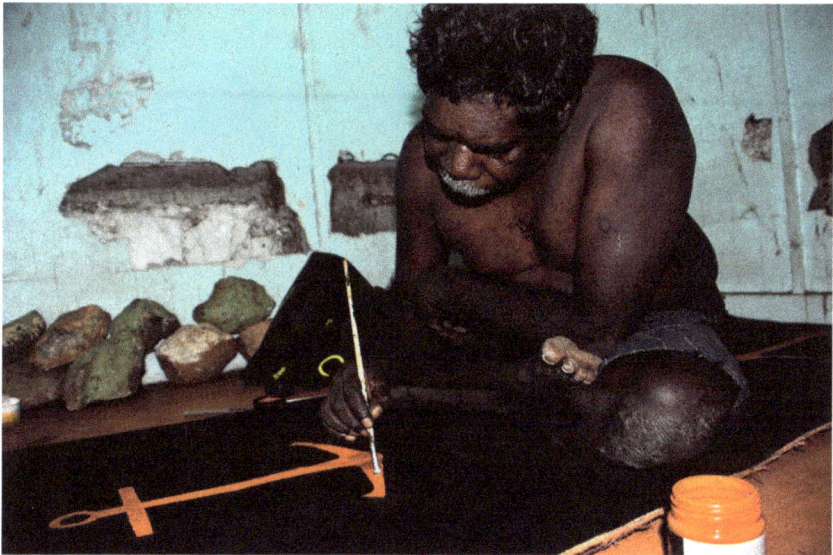

Figure 6.12: David Bukulatjpi painting *Djalkiri #1*, 2009.

As a Warramirri man he shares rights and responsibilities for the stories and images associated with Birrinydji. As Susan's sister's son, he was a close and trusted collaborator. This was the first bark he ever painted.

Source: Jennifer Deger.

The photograph above is exactly the kind of photograph that Yolngu never take. In every photo I have ever made with Yolngu, people have chosen to address themselves to the camera. In fact, often they look past the camera, past the particular moment and out to the future reciprocated gaze of family. Increasingly, I think, they look down the lens in anticipation of their death and its aftermath, a time when their relationships will live on through photographs.

When we source archival images from museums, family are often very disappointed when their ancestor does not look at the camera. This is interpreted as an expression of disapproval, not only of the anthropologist pointing the camera, but of the subsequent generations looking at them—looking for a connection with them—all these years later.

IMAGING IDENTITY

XIV

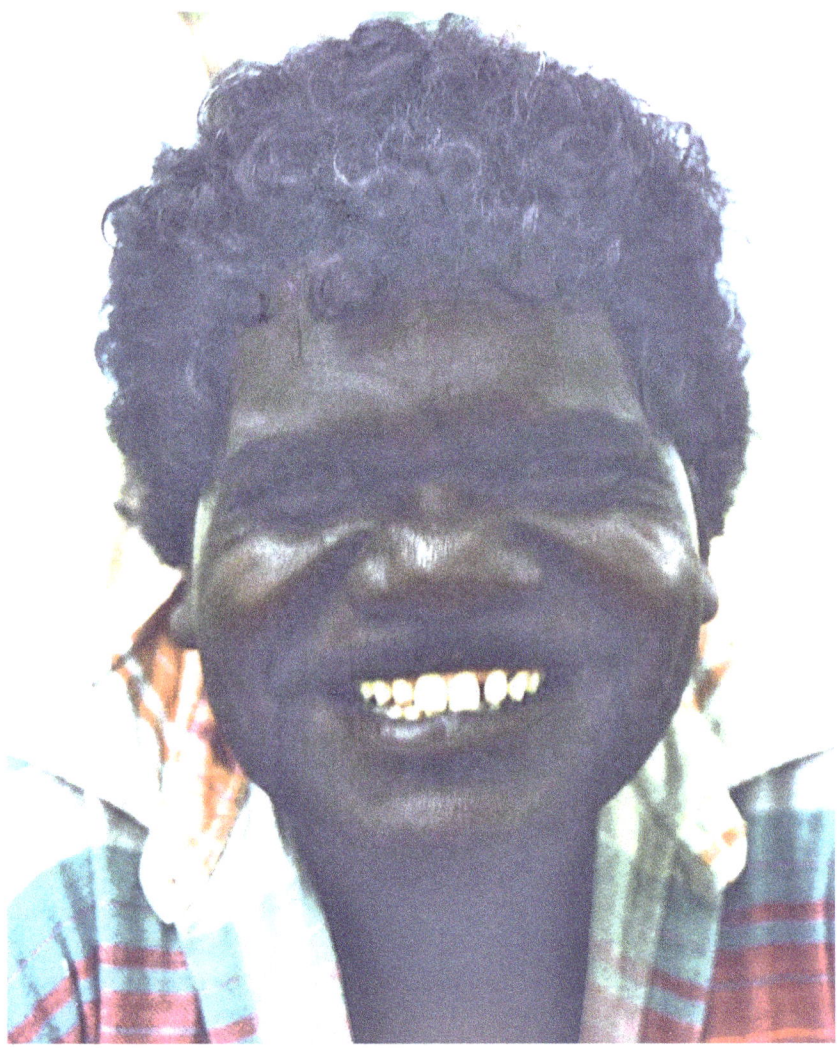

Figure 6.13: Portrait of Bangana Wunungmurra, date unknown.

Source: Jennifer Deger.

Of course not every family photo is a portrait. The image of Bangana repeating throughout was once simply a snapshot. It became a portrait when mobilised in some of the ways I have described: put into relationship with other images and figures so as to bring out and amplify qualities of character in ways that insistently illustrate and affirm the degree to which a Yolngu self is always constituted in and through relationships.

It occurs to me now that the image above became a portrait even before such projects of loving, insistent remediation. For surely this photo, along with every other image of Bangana where he is captured face on, looking outward to a future not yet imagined, became a portrait exactly in the moment he died: in the moment when the image became an uncanny facsimile of a figure no longer inhabiting fleshly human form. Herein lies a different yet equally wrenching encounter of self with self. One that must be recognised by those left behind.

XV

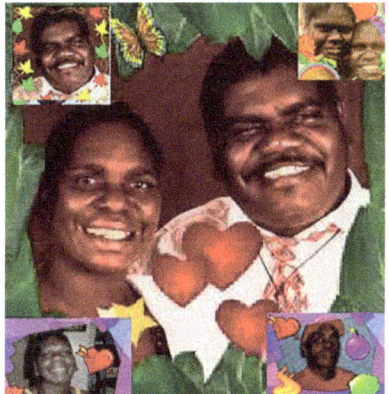

Figure 6.14: *ONLY.FAMILY*, Rowena Lay'pu Wunungmurra, 2010, phone-made jpeg.
Source: Courtesy of Miyarrka Media.

I am not the only one returning again and again to his face, his eyes and his image. Nor am I the only one mixing media in new ways. Lay'pu assembled this family collage on a mobile phone in 2011, the very making of the photo performing her missing him still, this affective labour shown by the multiple, overlapping hearts, a sentimentality tempered by the losses kept near to the surface. Other elements add to the layered meanings. The wreath of coloured leaves around Bangana's face in the top corner show him to be a reggae lover and serious smoker of marijuana. The leaves also stand in for an element of Dhalwangu identity featured in clan songs. Manjarr, a clan-specific song about a mangrove leaf, simultaneously gestures to images of mangrove leaves floating along in saltwater tides, and Bangana's fondness for smoking marijuana (something that Lay'pu also greatly enjoys, and in so doing, sees herself following in her father's footsteps).

These days, many young Yolngu assemble family portraits like these, often including photographs of the dead. They identify them as *gamanungu*, the same word they use for the designs painted on bark. Often they will add a soundtrack to such images, usually with specially selected *manikay* (clan songs).

XVI

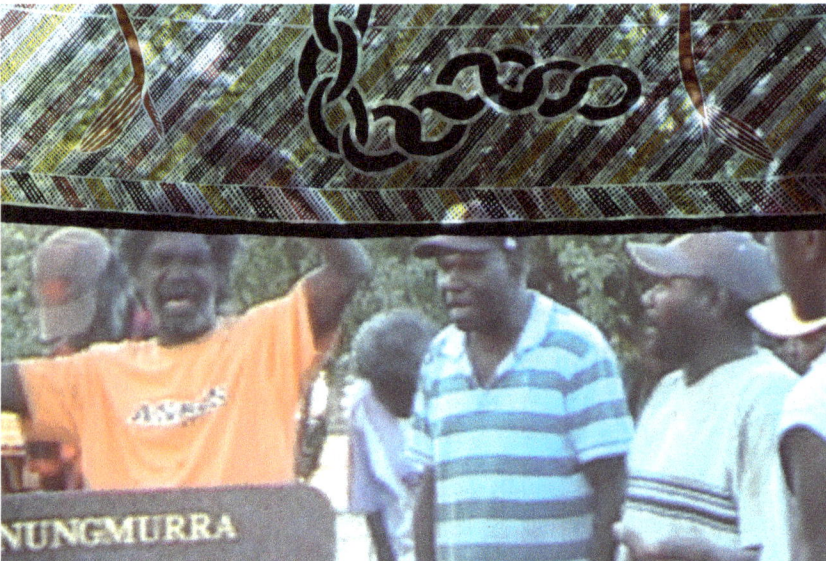

Figure 6.15: *Djalkiri #1* (close-up), during test projections, 2009.
Source: Jennifer Deger.

I like *Djalkiri #1* best when the video bleeds over the lines between the sections, though my Yolngu collaborators prefer the video to sit neatly in its frame, as originally intended. *Dhunupa* is the word they use to expresses an aesthetic concern with the work of making things straight. The pleasure and sense of correctness that comes from this is not driven by a strict and unbending desire for precision, nor by a sense that there is something intrinsically different about this video and its bark painting surrounds, but rather by a concern with attentively ordering things. Straightening something up is a performance of attention and due care, a way of putting things right.

XVII

The dynamics of encounter run deep in *Djalkiri #1*. In both form and content our work claims the transformative potential of intercultural incorporation. As digital sound and movement unsettle the usual sober rectitude of bark painting, our work confidently refuses simplistic categorical separations between 'old' and 'new' technologies or indeed 'them' and 'us'. Like the ritual projected on the bark, the work itself materialises foundational vectors of connection, incorporating the use of 'new' or 'foreign' technologies through a performative poetics of emplacement. While probably no one reading this will ever know the deep stories that lie under the crossed knives and long-chained anchors, what comes through strongly—to even the most casual visitor, I hope—is the confident audacity of the work. Perhaps this is what the digital most particularly adds in this context: a multi-sensorial energy palpably bringing new life to old forms.

When we installed our work in Sydney, we all agreed Bangana would have been pleased. Hanging prominently in a Balanda institution, this artwork is one for posterity: one that puffs its chest just a little, assuming its place on the wall, eyes to the future, uniquely distinctive and Yolngu in equal measure.

Certainly this is not portraiture as it matters to Nancy. The inner psychic disunities that compel his analysis do not interest Yolngu in the same ways. Instead, the gesture—whether in ritual, painting or photography—is towards an expanded and outward-orientated sense of becoming-in-relationship. This brings with it a very different sense of the self-to-self dynamics that make us who we are, and consequently a very different sense of the fault lines of fragility and hubris that, if exposed, might allow others to see the stuff from which we are really made.

If portraits compel us because of the ways they attend to the delicate and all-too-human relationships of selves encountering other selves, then this work both conforms to the definition and extends it.

By 'framing' contemporary life in relation to ancestral figures and actions, *Djalkiri #1* asserts—like all Yolngu art—that Yolngu selves extend far beyond individuated human form. Here the symbols of knives and anchors assert Bangana's identity and, by extension, his knowledge and power, as decisively as the books in Bronzino's *Portrait of Ugolino Martelli* do the same for that subject. Yet what makes this work unlike a 'traditional' bark painting—and thus arguably more like a portrait—is the way the pathos of the smiling human figure on the headstone undercuts the heroic postures painted directly on the bark. For those of us who live with the enduring fear, suspicion and blame that settled around the Djalkiri family in the wake of Bangana's death, this sense of human vulnerability as an integral aspect of claiming and wielding 'ancestral power' is a palpable dimension of the work. In a minor and manageable way, the work triggered these anxieties anew. Prior to commencing there were long discussions between us, as well as permissions sought from others, in order to ensure we were not committing any transgression in the use of the painted figures. The last thing any of us wanted was to stir things up again. And yet in a way it felt inevitable. And strangely proper. Bangana had always made it clear to me that in order to do such work—to publicly show who he was through the ways he used new media—would always be risking criticism and jealousy from others. The challenge, as he explained it to me, was to be as circumspect as possible in regard to the revelation of ancestral knowledge, while finding new forms and forums for it. In this way, he managed what I have called elsewhere a politics of presencing.[14]

Yet I too occupy a place within the bark, a fact often acknowledged by my collaborators, who, despite their interest and critical help in making sure the work satisfied all Yolngu social and aesthetic criteria, saw this artwork ultimately as my project. (Like the photograph on the gravestone, the BarkTV remains a one-off. There has been no interest in pushing this mixed-media further, although we have experimented with other forms of bark projection.) Assuming my place as filmmaker-anthropologist-adopted clan member—often when I film I am encouraged to come closer than the other women, for the sake of the recording—my point of view frames and fills the middle panel.

---

14   See Deger, 2006.

In doing so it invokes a shared history of media-making, locating this work within a trajectory of innovation and experiment begun when we were all young together.

And so *Djalkiri #1* materialises the verve and genius located not in individuals, nor even necessarily cultures, but in the foundational relationships that make us who we are—and who we might become. Although lacking the kind of recognisable immediacy generally expected from a portrait, this ethnographic experiment offers an encounter with an expanded sense of what it means to be human: an encounter less concerned with the fleshiness of figures or the fragile markings of individual character than with the pulsing substrates that extend beyond and beneath the span of a single life.

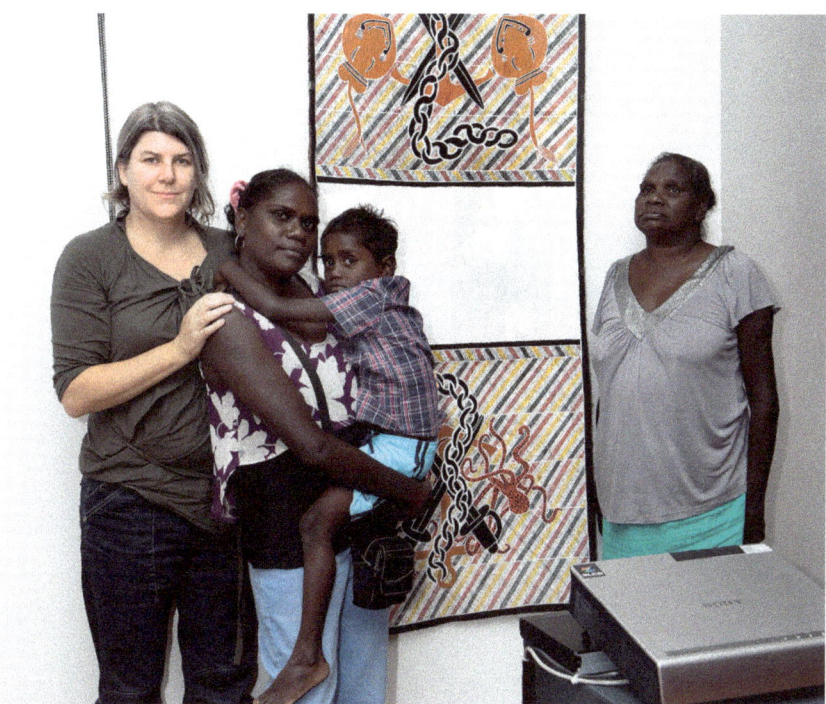

Figure 6.16: Jennifer Deger, Samantha Yawulwuy Wunungmurra, Antonnio Gurrururu Wanambi, Susan Marrawakamirr Marrawungu, Macquarie University Art Gallery 2009.
Source: Courtesy of Macquarie University Art Gallery.

Acknowledgements

Many thanks especially to Marrawakamirr Marrawungu, Yawulwuy Wunungmurra, David Bukulatjpi, Wapit Munungurr and Yangipuy Wanambi for all their input into the exhibition and my understandings of it. The Djalkiri family have generously given permission for the use of the photographs and images that appear in this chapter. Much gratitude also to Jane Sloan, Melinda Hinkson and Alison Leitch for reading unwieldy early drafts; and again to Melinda Hinkson for her invitation to think about our work in these ways. I am grateful especially to Greg Downey and Rhonda Davis at Macquarie University for their energetic support of the *interventions* exhibition. An Australian Research Council Postdoctoral Fellowship and a Future Fellowship supported the research that eventually resulted in this essay. Finally, I am grateful for the support of the Cairns Institute at James Cook University.

Index

9/11 10, 47, 111

Aboriginal
    painting styles 119n5, 124n10, 124n11
    see also Yolngu
absence 7, 35, 38, 51, 60, 62, 63, 66, 73, 74, 76, 77
abstraction, technological xvii, 7, 10, 32, 51–53, 56, 115, 116
acknowledgement 6, 15, 21–24, 25–27, 28, 31, 32, 35–36, 70, 74
    see also Rembrandt
Adorno, Theodor 9, 89, 90, 93
advertising 2, 87
anthropology 122, 124, 130, 132, 138, 144
Appadurai, Arjun 37
Archibald Prize 39
Arnhem Land *see* Yolngu
art
    anti-art 87
    as agency 8, 62
    as creating objects of knowledge 56
    criticism as a form of 90
    of making an identity 37
    as mode of thinking 62, 64
    as relational 65, 79, 80, 117–118,
        see also encounter
    see also representation
art criticism 17–18, 29
Art Gallery of NSW 40

Astruc, Alexandre 86, 91
authenticity
    and portraiture 63–64, 65, 79, 81
    and representation 39–42
    in scientific images 105, 107
    see also truth
autobiography 4, 8
    and *caméra-stylo* 85–88, 92–93, 97–100
    see also portraiture

Barthes, Roland 70, 77n31
Bauman, Zygmunt 37, 60
becoming, and identity 7, 61, 80, 123, 137, 139
belonging 8, 60, 61, 62, 63, 65, 81, 129
Belting, Hans 38, 49
Benjamin, Walter 89, 93
binarism 38, 56, 86, 90
bioinformatics 103, 110–115
    see also faciality
biopolitics 4–5, 10, 103–116
Bois, Yves-Alain 40–41, 94
boundary-crossing *also* border crossing 86, 79, 91, 93, 95
Brah, Avtar 62, 79, 80
Bronzino, Angelo 24–25, 119–120, 138
Buck-Morss, Susan 64, 79
Butor, Michel 96

141

caméra-stylo see film and video essay
capitalism 40–41
  see also late capitalism
Castiglione, Baldassare 21, 29
Cervantes 21
Chiu, Melissa 66
Cixous, Hélène 64–65
collage 87, 90, 96, 99, 135
Colless, Edward 66, 68
computers 5, 38, 54, 93, 97, 110, 131
  see also digital
copy, the 17, 40, 64–69, 77, 80
  simulacrum 4
  simulation 40, 112
  see also photocopy, and representation
critical theory 46, 85, 86
cross-cultural 5, 10, 11, 53, 129, 131, 137

Daney, Serge 85
Darwin, Charles 9, 101, 103–108, 110, 111, 114, 115
David, Jacques-Louis 24
da Vinci, Leonardo 15
de Certeau, Michel 88
Degas, Edgar 49
de Hooch, Pieter 27
Deleuze, Gilles 10, 89, 94, 110
Descartes, *also* Cartesian rationalism 21, 22, 97
diaspora
  displacement 8, 60, 63, 65, 76
  identification 61–62
  and representation 5, 7, 8, 59–81
  theory and experience 59–61, 86
diasporic consciousness 72, 81
digital
  aesthetic 111
  age 2, 10, 16, 37–43, 55–56, 65, 93

  technology 3, 5–6, 8, 10, 16, 43, 49, 64, 85, 89, 110, 111, 123, 126, 128, 129, 137
Dou, Gerrit 27
drawing, as distinctive practice 6, 8, 19, 49, 57, 71, 73, 76, 77, 80
Duchenne de Boulogne, Guillaume 9–10, 101–108, 110, 114
Dupain, Max 44

Ekeman, Paul and Friesen, Warren 111–116
emotion
  in art criticism 11, 17
  in act of painting 8, 9, 51
emotions, the
  typology of 9, 10, 101–116
  see also face, the
encounter, through the portrait 5–6, 15–36, 47, 89, 117–118, 119, 135, 137, 139
ethnography *see* anthropology
European art traditions 4, 8, 63, 65, 66, 79, 90, 119–120
  see also representation
expression *see* emotion, and face, the

face, the 2, 3, 4, 6, 10, 60, 65, 66, 118, 121
  and identity 24–29, 32
  and imaginative projection 18–20
  and moral attitude *see* encounter
  photography compared to painting 32–35
  and reputation 22–23
Facial Action Coding System 112
facial expression 101–108, 111–116
facial recognition 3, 10, 16, 103–116
faciality 101, 109–116
family portraits *see* photography
Farber, Manny 88
feeling *see* emotions, the
film essay *see* video essay
film noir 88

INDEX

flesh 19, 25, 31, 32, 34, 51, 53, 135, 139
Foucault, Michel 111
Fuller, Buckminster 95, 96

Gadamer, Hans-Georg 4
Genet, Jean 34, 94–95
Glasheen, Michael 95
globalisation 59–60, 92, 93
Godard, Jean-Luc 86, 91–92, 96
governmentality 3, 4, 9
  see also biopolitics
Guattari, Félix 10, 110,

Hall, Stuart 7, 60–61
Hals, Frans 25, 27
Hirsch, Marianne 69–70
Holocaust 70
Horn, Roni 64–65

identification 7, 11, 61–62, 69–70, 74, 80, 81
identity
  bourgeois identity 26–32
  contemporary identity 37–39, 101, 110–116
  cultural identity 59
  and the interpersonal 16, 21–25
  personal identity 3, 6, 7, 20, 62, 63, 101, 103
  see also self, the
  see also diaspora
image, the 2, 11, 12, 17, 18, 35, 38, 64, 65–69
  image culture 2–11, 55–56, 86–87, 114–115
  see also digital, and moving image technologies
imagination 8, 9, 15, 37, 51, 64
individualism 3, 21, 22, 37–38, 62
intercultural *see* cross-cultural
intersubjectivity 5, 7, 10, 16, 113, 117–118
  see also encounter
Italian city states 23–24

JanMohamed, Abul R 95

Kant, Emmanuel 21

late capitalism 2, 55–57, 93
Leach, Sam 39–40, 41–43, 56
Lee, Lindy 8, 65–68,
Levi-Strauss, Claude 56
likeness 15–16, 18, 20, 25, 29, 31, 34–35, 118, 121, 126
Locke, John 21
Lukacs, Georg 9, 90

Marker, Chris 86, 91, 92–93, 98
memory 9, 72, 86, 87, 88, 92, 93
  see also postmemory
migration 59–60
  interior emigration 8, 88–89
  see also diaspora
Mirzoeff, Nicholas 63
Mitchell, WJT 10, 43, 55
mixed media 119, 121, 135, 138–139
mobile phones 5
  mobile phone art 135
modernity 3–4, 6, 21–24, 37–38, 40, 89, 96, 99, 100, 103, 131
Mondrian 41
Montaigne, Michel 8, 87, 89–90
moving image technologies 92, 94, 113, 114, 116
  see also video essay
mutuality, in portraiture 6–7, 25, 32, 118

Nancy, Jean-Luc 5, 11–12, 117–118, 120, 137
National Portrait Gallery 1–2, 3
nature 46, 53
neoliberalism 10
  see also governmentality
neuroscience 101, 102–108
new media 9, 39–42, 54, 85–87, 89, 92, 94, 97, 99, 110, 138
  see also mixed media, and digital

143

other, the 5, 6, 15–16, 18, 20, 21–29, 60, 73, 87, 88, 117–118
see also encounter, and intersubjective

pastiche 9, 10
painting
    bark painting 121, 137, 138
    as distinctive practice 5, 6–7, 21, 29, 31–32, 38, 41, 43, 53, 57
    as producing objects 17
    in wider visual culture 40–43, 47, 51, 54–56
    see also representation
Peters, John Durham 54–55
Petit, Charles 89
perception 15, 46, 54, 103, 114
performance art 86–87, 94, 99
personhood 5, 7, 10, 16, 21, 23, 80, 104
    see also self, and subjectivity
photocopy 8, 65–69, 73, 77, 80
photography 3, 5, 6, 7, 8, 9, 11, 16, 32–34, 41, 64, 69, 71, 73, 77, 104, 105, 106, 107, 115, 123
    and Aboriginal notions of death and the sacred 122–124, 131–136
    art photography 105
    digital photography 16
    see also digital
    family album photography 69, 125
    mediating painting process 43–46, 49–51
    and science 102–115
place 11, 39, 52, 54, 61, 72, 130, 137
Portia Geach Memorial Award 47
portraiture
    animals in 7, 51–52
    as autobiographical form see self-portraiture
    depicting character 103–104, 115, 118, 121, 139
    as European art form see Bronzino, and representation
    future in 60–63, 96, 133–135, 137
    morality in 6, 15, 20, 32, 33
    in profile 28
    in relation to celebrity and the nation 2
    and subjectivity 6, 15
    see also diaspora
    as relational 53, 65, 73, 76, 77, 79, 80, 81, 125
    see also encounter
    see also self-portraiture
postmemory 69–70, 80
postmodern, the 34, 85, 86, 94, 96
presence 31, 32, 38, 55–56, 60–61, 63, 64, 66, 73, 74, 79, 81
Prodger, Phillip 105, 107
profiling 114–115
public/private spheres 2, 21, 22, 26, 70
Pynacker, Adam 39, 42

Raphael 26, 29
recognition see acknowledgement
Rembrandt 16–19, 21–23
Renaissance 15, 24, 65
representation 8, 17, 35
    and the child 18–20
    contemporary practices of 10, 51, 54, 60
    as enactment and thinking through 80–81, 105
    politics of 34, 40–43, 90–92, 94
    see also biopolitics
reproducibility 41, 64, 65, 66, 74, 105
Richter, Gerhardt 51
Richter, Hans 90
Rubens 27
Rushdie, Salman 93

Sayers, Andrew xiii
science 56, 111, 115
    see also neuroscience
securitisation 10, 101, 108, 111, 113, 114, 115
self, the 4, 5, 21–22, 26, 29, 97, 118, 60, 73, 118, 132
    selfies 32
    see also subjectivity, and identity
self-portraiture 8, 26–34, 47, 69, 73
    see also autobiography, and Rembrandt
Serres, Michel 89, 97
Shakespeare 21, 22
sitter, the 4, 6, 7, 15–16, 21, 25, 27, 31, 35, 72–74, 77, 107
Snow, CP 95, 97
social/cultural transformation 4, 6, 23–24, 27, 59, 103
social mobility 22–23
Steen, Jan 27
studio, the 7, 21, 44, 46, 47, 49, 55, 73, 74
subjectivity 4, 6, 8, 10, 15, 24, 28, 55, 80, 90, 93, 99
    of the artist 7, 49, 55
    diasporic subjectivity 59–81
    of the sitter 15
surveillance *see* biopolitics, and securitisation

technological change 3–11, 37, 122
    see also digital and new media
technological mediation 2, 6, 10, 37–40, 43
    and Aboriginal culture 119–139
    in painting 41–51, 53, 55, 57
television 32, 43, 91, 95
theological-aristocratic age 24–26
Thompson, John 37–38
Titian 28, 29
truth
    and the face 104, 108, 112–115
    in representation 10, 65, 79

Väliaho, Pasi 10
van Alpen, Ernst 4, 62
Vermeer 27
video 6, 49, 101, 104, 112, 113, 121, 122, 124, 130
video essay 8–9, 85–100
Virilio, Paul 113
visual culture 56, 57, 63

Warhol, Andy 33–34
Wynne Prize 39, 40, 41

Yolngu 5, 53, 119–139

Zurbrugg, Nicholas 94

www.ingramcontent.com/pod-product-compliance
Lightning Source LLC
Chambersburg PA
CBHW040522220526
45473CB00026B/2937